"The Stonington Tragedy"
Murder at Darling Hill

Judith G. duPont

Ramsbotham
Editions
THE STONINGTON HISTORICAL SOCIETY

The Stonington Historical Society, Inc.
Stonington, CT 06378

© 2007 by Judith G. duPont
All rights reserved.

Published 2007, 2010
Published in the United States of America

Book design by Marie Carija

Photographs by Barbara Holland, Judith duPont, and from the archives of the Stonington Historical Society

Library of Congress Cataloging-in-Publication Data

DuPont, Judith G. (Judith Gildersleeve)
The Stonington tragedy : murder at Darling Hill / Judith G. duPont.
p. cm.
Includes bibliographical references.
ISBN 978-0-9794013-6-7 (alk. paper)
1. Murder–Connecticut–Stonington–Case studies. 2. Stonington (Conn.)–History–19th century. I. Stonington Historical Society. II. Title.
HV6534.S76D87 2010
364.152'3097465–dc22
2010033829

PREFACE

The Langworthy murder story fell into my lap. Several years ago, as I was sorting through family books to give away, a neatly folded, yellowed newspaper article dropped out of an old volume. The book didn't seem to have any value, but the article's headline riveted my attention: "Another Connecticut Tragedy—Double Murder in Stonington." This detailed account from the April 25, 1874, edition of the *Hartford Times* was like no Stonington story that I had ever heard before. A grisly murder that occurred in 1874 was far removed from the proud history of the town's founding in 1649 or from the tales of illustrious defenders in the 1814 Battle of Stonington. I saved the article and discarded the book. After many years, I found the time to look into the facts behind the so-called "double murder." The opportunity to uncover something forgotten in Stonington's past was as intriguing to me as solving the murder mystery.

Initially, I found the murder story totally absorbing, especially after discovering the trial testimony in the *New London Evening Telegram*. The accounts of that dark April night, complete with pools of blood, barking dogs, and strangers on the road, are classic and bring to mind other legendary murder mysteries, both fictional and real. In truth, it was difficult to resist the urge to follow my imagination into the realm of fiction when confronted with such a sensational scenario. But the drama inherent in the documents I found in my research is compelling enough to stand alone, and I concluded that the story should be told as it really happened, without any invention.

As the saga of the Langworthy family came to light, it did prove to be quintessentially a Stonington story. It relies heavily on place, the majestic Darling Hill overlooking Long Island Sound, as well as a landscape of coves, fields, rocks, and dirt roads. The connections, both physical and political, between the country town and its subdivision, the bustling Borough of Stonington, reveal a tension that continues to this day. The family members and the townsfolk—some of them descendants of the town's founding fathers—had all put down deep roots in this section of Connecticut, earning their livelihoods, attending church, and cultivating a strong sense of loyalty to the community. These people are not the usual heroes of pageants or history books, but they seem somehow familiar. The hardscrabble farms, the railroad, shops on Water Street, the road to Mystic, and classic churches confirm that the setting is certainly Stonington.

Nonetheless, it is one thing to be able to relate to location, but quite something else to understand the inhabitants of a particular historical period. As I read through the newspaper reports, Jerome Anderson's editorials in the *Stonington Mirror*, and the trial testimony, I realized that these documents provided a unique opportunity, that of hearing the family and its neighbors express themselves in their own words. We hear Henry Langworthy struggling to recall his various hired hands, and his wife, Maria, describing her kitchen and correcting the lawyers. Where else would we ever hear from someone like Constable Tillinghast, the reluctant detective, or the methodical Dr. Brayton? Some of the lively comments made at town and Borough meetings have been preserved, including the fact that Thomas Palmer, who wanted to "knock" the suspect in the head, had some difficulty with spelling and punctuation. The long accounts of neighbors crossing the cove or walking home at the end of the day provided "a shadow of a doubt" for the defense, but today they recreate what it was like to live along Quiambaug Cove 130 years ago.

Our most intimate knowledge of the past generally comes from first person accounts such as diaries and letters. But in this case news reporting fulfills that function, and, to our benefit, includes a wide representation of the local population. Interestingly, the defendant's own testimony describes in a straightforward manner what it was like to work on a Connecticut farm in the 1870s. And, the responses of Courtland Langworthy give us a small inkling of how it felt to be handicapped in the late nineteenth century.

The people we encounter in this Langworthy family history come from all walks of life and provide a means of examining the changing economic and social realities in Connecticut after the Civil War. While land was always the primary basis for the Langworthys' wealth, Henry Langworthy also invested in ships. His college-educated son, however, bought stock in a factory building company. Ironically, the Langworthy family facilitated the building of the railroad and the highway, symbols of the period's rapid economic expansion and of the simultaneous decline of Henry Langworthy's kind of farming. Over three generations, Langworthy men serve as representatives of significant social movements of their day, Samuel as a Baptist deacon, Henry as a temperance proponent, and Hamilton as a fraternal society member.

Conflict between landed family members and their laborers is at the center of this story, but as the years go by it is increasingly evident that both land owners and laborers found it difficult to earn a living on a small farm. Henry Langworthy's long list of hired hands presents an invaluable and possibly overlooked record of the unstable employment conditions on farms in the 1870s.

With his engineering background, Hamilton Langworthy seems all too ready to leave dairy farming behind. Neither of his Uncle Samuel's daughters settled on their family land, which was eventually partly developed into a summer community. Thus, by the close of the century, we see the effects of the vogue for summer residences on the small farming and maritime community—a new class of investor as well as a new source of wealth.

The research involved in the Langworthy story proved to be extensive. I followed the trail starting with the *Hartford Times* article (which turned out to be filled with errors) through other newspapers, land records, church records, probate and tax records. I checked every Stonington-based history book as well as some on Connecticut history and interviewed family members. At the mention of Lewiston and Auburn, Maine, in connection with William Libby, I was in the car and was able to drive down No Name Pond Road in search of the Libby house. My greatest disappointment came when, at the Connecticut State Library, I discovered the folder containing the trial papers was empty. Apparently, the papers were missing as far back as the 1930s, when trial records were catalogued. The most meaningful research for me took place on and around Darling Hill. Driving along the cove at dusk, staring up at the hill and trying to picture the fields with only rocks and a few cedar trees, searching for traces of the old bridge, I tried to wipe away the new and settle myself in the older landscape.

One ancillary aspect of the research is worth noting simply because it is rarely brought out in our local histories. At the time of the Langworthy murder only nine years had elapsed since the end of the Civil War. I kept running into references to the Civil War and the war records of various individuals connected to the story. The Stonington Langworthys were either too old or too young to serve in the war, but Henry Langworthy's brother

George had a son who spent two years in the 8th Connecticut Volunteers; Lieutenant Joseph Chadwick Langworthy fought in the Battle of Antietam and died in Virginia of diphtheria in 1863. The newspaperman John Tibbits attained the rank of major and was wounded at Antietam, and Marvin Wait, son of the prosecuting attorney, John T. Wait, lost his life at Antietam. The head of the Mystic Valley Institute, John Bucklyn, was always referred to as "captain" out of respect for his Civil War service. And probably Samuel Tillinghast had been made constable thanks to his having served in the war. Far from the battlefields and years later, the Civil War exerted an influence on this part of Connecticut, and we are repeatedly reminded of that fact in the Langworthy story.

The history of this particular Langworthy family involved far more than the events of one dark night in April 1874, and I could not have done the research or written this book without the patient assistance of several people. First, Susan Hart, the great-granddaughter of Matilda and Hamilton Langworthy, has been supportive of this project from the beginning. My thanks go to her for allowing me to delve into her family's history and for making photographs and letters available. I am also very grateful to Susan Knox, whose memories and photographs of Darling Hill were invaluable resources. When it came to doing the research, Mary Thacher, former town historian, helped me understand how and where to find many of the records. And I thank her for sharing material on Stonington buildings and on Lydia Fellowes, as well. Anne Tate, Scotty Breed, and Robert Farwell at the Stonington Historical Society's Woolworth Library were always welcoming, and they cheerfully made their resources available to me. The newspaper collection at the New London Country Historical Society was essential, and I can't thank the librarians there enough for allowing me to come day after day to transcribe text. Others who helped me answer some very puzzling questions were Jeannie Sherman and the reference staff in the Historical and Genealogical Section of the Connecticut State Library; Michael Lord at the Androscoggin County Historical Society in Auburn, Maine; the reference staffs at the Lewiston Public Library and the Auburn Public Library in Maine, and the reference staff at the Mystic Seaport library and Don Treworgy, the planetarium supervisor at the Seaport. I would also like to thank the diligent volunteers at the Mystic River Historical Society. Finally, this book would not have been possible without the encouragement and editorial skills of James Boylan and Betsy Wade.

Judith G. duPont
June 2007

"Mr. and Mrs. Langworthy have known peculiar joys and peculiar sorrow [and] through all their trials have borne themselves with Christian patience, and now, in the fast thickening twilight of life, are awaiting the summons to join those 'gone before' in the land where all mysteries are explained and the ills of life remembered no more."

Hurd, ed., History of New London County *(1882)*.

1. Mystery and Rumors

Today, driving through southeastern Connecticut on Route 1 from Stonington to Mystic, we pass Wamphassuc Road to the south, gather speed up the hill, and leave Montauk Avenue and Lords Hill Road behind. The panoramic view of Quiambaug Cove and Fishers Island Sound spreads out before us as we rush downhill, over the cove, and on toward Mystic.

Had this modern two-lane section of highway existed in the mid-1800s, it would have sliced right through the farm of Henry Davis Langworthy. An 1868 map of the town of Stonington shows Langworthy's property situated on top of Darling Hill. While some have speculated that the hill was christened 'Darling' in honor of a Langworthy wife, others have claimed that Indians were originally responsible for the name, uncharacteristic as it sounds. In any event, Darling Hill remains a prominent feature of Stonington's landscape.

The Langworthy family lived on Darling Hill for nearly a century, but their story takes us off the modern highway and onto small dirt roads and pentways, into farmhouses and barns, to meet people who lived and worked in a Stonington we can only faintly recognize today.

• **Mystery and Rumors**

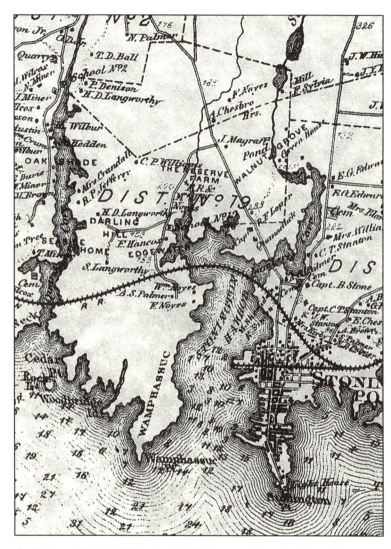

On 1868 map, Darling Hill is at middle left, Stonington Borough on lower right.

Mystery and Rumors • 7

The Langworthy tract was only one of the numerous large farms dotting the town's many districts from Pawcatuck on the east to Mystic on the west and extending north to the North Stonington line.[1] While seafaring and shipbuilding come to mind first when we think of Stonington, farming had sustained the town's rural population since the original settlement in the mid-1600s, and holdings of more than a hundred acres were not unusual well into the nineteenth century. However, the post-Civil War environment steadily brought changes. From a peak in 1860, Connecticut's acreage of improved land steadily declined as the century came to a close. The familiar Currier & Ives engravings of peaceful Connecticut farmyards may have been sentimental favorites, but they represented an all too fleeting scene, even in rural Stonington. And on Darling Hill, the Langworthy family was called upon repeatedly to defend its peace as well as its acreage.

Darling Hill was Henry Langworthy's realm. In fact, after extensively remodeling his father's house there in the mid-1800s, he dubbed it "Farmer's Palace." Henry's parents, Samuel and Ethelinda Davis Langworthy, settled on Darling Hill (north of the present Route 1) in the mid-1820s. They brought with them their three sons—Samuel Jr., born in 1797 in Hopkinton, Rhode Island; George, born in 1807 in Connecticut; and Henry, also born in Connecticut, in 1809.[2]

---

1   F.W. Beers, A.D. Ellis, and G.G. Soule, *Atlas of New London County* (New York, 1868).

2   Samuel Langworthy was born on September 11, 1771, in Hopkinton, Rhode Island, son of Samuel Langworthy (1745-1818) and Mercy Saunders; he married Ethelinda Davis (born June 7, 1767, daughter of Joseph and Mary Davis of Westerly, Rhode Island) on July 13, 1796. They moved from Rhode Island—first to Old Mystic and then to Darling Hill, Stonington. In addition to three sons, they had two daughters—Ethelinda, who died in 1806 at the age of five, and Tacy, who died in 1804 at the age of one. William Franklin Langworthy, *The Langworthy Families in America* (Hamilton, N.Y.: Tuttle, 1940).

8 • Mystery and Rumors

Samuel Langworthy was a farmer, a Democrat, and a deacon in the Baptist Church, "a thoroughly good man."[3] After moving from Hopkinton, Rhode Island, to Connecticut around 1802, Samuel purchased 195 acres of land in 1814 from George Haley "near the head of Mistick," in what we now call Old Mystic, for $6,000.[4] Less than ten years later, he bought 150 acres, with buildings, from Samuel F. Denison for $9,000. The land, bordered on the west by Quiambog Cove and on the south by "the salt water of Fisher's Island Sound," covered the top of Darling Hill and stretched east to the Palmer property on Wamphassuc Point.

During the 1830s, Deacon Langworthy added to his Darling Hill farm by purchasing an eight-acre wood lot from the estate of James Dean, fifty acres along Quiambog Cove from Lodowick Denison, and a parcel of three and a half acres to the north from the heirs of David C. Smith.[5] Thus, Langworthy's entire holding covered both sides of the hill, including what we now know as Lord's Point and extending north to the land on the west side of Montauk Avenue. The broad, high hill provided sweeping stretches for grazing pastures, hay fields, and orchards, an auspicious setting for the Langworthys' dairy farm.

On November 20, 1835, Ethelinda Davis Langworthy died "after a long and distressing illness." Deacon Samuel lost no time. That "very evening after her funeral" he proposed marriage to Lydia Fellows, the daughter of Deacon Elnathan Fellows of

---

3   D. Hamilton Hurd, *History of New London County, Connecticut*...(Philadelphia, J.W. Lewis & Co., 1882), p. 727.

4   Town of Stonington Land Records, vol. 16, pp. 236, 237, 598.

5   Town of Stonington Land Records, vol. 17, pp. 308, 585; vol. 18, p. 337; vol. 19, pp. 129, 175. "Quiambog" was the spelling commonly used in the nineteenth century.

Main Street in Stonington Borough.[6] Despite an age difference of almost twenty years, Lydia decided to accept the sixty-four-year-old Samuel's proposal. Less than eight weeks later, on January 12, 1836, the two were married, and Deacon Langworthy moved to the Borough, leaving his youngest son, Henry, to live in his house on Darling Hill. Henry's eldest brother, Samuel Jr., who had married Prudence Chesebrough in 1823, built a farmhouse in 1835 on the southern part of the hill, overlooking Cedar (Lord's) Point and Fishers Island Sound. The middle Langworthy brother, George, remained on the Old Mystic property.

After moving to the Borough, Deacon Langworthy sold his three smaller pieces of land to Samuel Jr. and Henry for $1,700, about $400 less than he paid for them. In 1846, when Deacon Langworthy was seventy-five, he officially deeded all the former Denison property on Darling Hill to his two sons living there.[7] The southern portion of approximately one hundred and forty acres was transferred to Samuel Jr., and the northern section of one hundred acres went to Henry. Both properties included shore privileges such as the rights to seaweed and oyster beds in Quiambog Cove. According to the Stonington land records, the two sons were obligated to "grant, lease and farm let" the properties back to their father for his lifetime.[8] Although the original

---

6   Rev. Amos Chesebrough, "Stonington in Days of Yore, Part II," *Historical Footnotes,* 23 (May 1986), p. 2.

7   Town of Stonington Land Records, vol. 22, pp. 163, 164, 165. Deacon Langworthy also deeded the 193-acre Old Mystic property to his son George.

8   Town of Stonington Land Records, vol. 22, pp. 402, 403, 404. Deacon Samuel Langworthy died on September 6, 1853. In 1854, the three Langworthy sons paid Lydia F. Langworthy $400 to discharge her claim to an annuity set up under the terms of a prenuptial agreement with the deacon. They also relinquished any claim to a barn that their father had built on Lydia's land in Stonington Borough. Stonington Probate Records, vol. 18, p. 429. A reference in Lydia Langworthy's diary (January 1, 1854) indicates that she did not get along with Henry Langworthy or his wife and wished that their religion would "bring them terrible repentance." The text of Deacon Langworthy's will and probate inventory are printed as an appendix on page 140.

deed from Samuel F. Denison specified one hundred and fifty acres, these later deeds total two hundred and forty acres, and it is unknown whether more land was acquired or whether there was a discrepancy in the record or the survey.

HENRY DAVIS LANGWORTHY'S early life was not unlike that of many Connecticut farmers in the years before the Civil War. He received a common school education, at the small district schools in Stonington. Influenced by his family, he joined the Baptist Church in Mystic when he was thirteen and remained a member for fifty-eight years.[9] In 1831, at the age of twenty-two, he served briefly as a captain in the "Old Road" local militia. As a young man, he tried his hand at being a merchant in Mystic for two years but gave it up in favor of farming the Darling Hill land. He "steadily held to the Democratic principles of his ancestors,"[10] the same principles championing farmers, laborers, and the common man so emblematic of the era's Jacksonian Democracy.

Three years after his father left Darling Hill, Henry, aged thirty, decided to marry, and chose his eighteen-year-old first cousin Maria Pierce Clarke. Maria's mother, Elizabeth Langworthy, was a younger sister of Henry's father, Deacon Samuel Langworthy. Elizabeth had married Russell Clarke, a farmer, and they had a dozen children, including Maria and her twin sis-

---

[9] In 1861, the Second and Third Baptist churches in Mystic joined to form the Union Baptist Church, which sits on the hill overlooking West Main Street. Church records show that for unexplained reasons Henry Langworthy, his wife Maria, and daughter were "excluded" in the early 1860s for a short period.

[10] Hurd, ed., *History of New London County*, p. 727.

ter Mary Taylor, who were born in Lebanon, Connecticut.[11] Henry Langworthy and Maria Pierce Clarke were married on September 29, 1839, and the following summer their first child, Henry Courtland, was born. A daughter, named Ethelinda for her grandmother, arrived on September 8, 1841, and two years later another daughter, Anna Maria, was born, only to die eleven weeks later. On June 16, 1845, the Langworthys' second son, James Hamilton, was born. Soon thereafter, Henry, having been deeded the Darling Hill property, "took down the old house and built about it, living in various parts of it at the same time, until he had made a fine country house called the 'Farmer's Palace,'" as Stonington's chronicler Grace Wheeler put it.[12] On August

Farmer's Palace after the Langworthy era

---

11   Elizabeth Langworthy (1790-1871) was the third wife of Russell Clarke. Their twins, Mary and Maria, were born April 18, 1821. The Clarkes later moved to Newport. *Westerly Sun*, October 16, 1899.

12   Grace Denison Wheeler, *Homes of Our Ancestors in Stonington, Conn.* (Salem, Mass.: 1903), pp. 106-107.

16, 1856, when Maria was thirty-five and Henry forty-seven, the Langworthy's youngest child was born. The boy, Irvin Newton, became the delight of his older siblings and loving parents. The family was complete, and the Darling Hill farm, as well as Henry's fortunes, flourished.

THAT HARBINGER of the industrial age, the railroad, soon pushed its way into the agricultural setting bordering Quiambog Cove. In the summer of 1857, Henry Langworthy and his

Quiambog Cove in the nineteenth century, looking north

brother Samuel each sold strips of land to the New Haven, New London, & Stonington Railroad Company for the completion of the track route from the ferry landing on the Thames River in Groton to Stonington Borough, thence to Boston. Henry Langworthy received $315 for his portion, 99 feet wide and almost a quarter of a mile long. This piece cut through his land in the area between the Alexander Palmer farm on Wamphassuc Point and Cedar (Lords) Point. Samuel's portion ran almost a half-mile from Henry's line to Quiambog Cove with provisions for two stone culverts, and the elder Langworthy brother was paid $750 for this larger piece of land. Both deeds allowed for "convenient crossings with cattle guards" at certain strategic spots to provide access to land south of the tracks.[13]

Henry and Maria Langworthy seemed to believe that a sound education would equip their children to handle the economic challenges that they, quite literally, saw on their horizon. After attending the Quiambog District school on Cove Road, the two older boys were sent away to study. In the fall of 1860, Maria Langworthy wrote to Courtland, "We are delighted to hear that you are doing nicely in your studies. You must persevere and try to improve every opportunity that is shown you." She also noted that four-year-old Irvin "wants to see Corty." Courtland received a "Reward of Merit" card inscribed with the maxim "Ambition is the ladder to fame." Hamilton traveled to Troy, New York, to attend Rensselaer Polytechnic Institute, and graduated in July 1865, just three months after the end of the Civil War, with a degree in civil engineering. A photograph shows him looking urbane and comfortable among his twenty-six classmates.[14] It is uncertain how much early education the daughter, Ethelinda, received outside the house on Darling Hill, but when she was a teenager her family elected to send her away to study, rather than enroll her at the nearby Wadawanuck Young Ladies Institute in Stonington. Ethelinda entered the Music Vale Seminary in Salem, Connecticut.

Music Vale, which was established in 1833, had a fine reputation and attracted female students from throughout the United States, including the ante-bellum South.[15] The young women of the school were expected to participate in monthly concerts

---

13 Town of Stonington Land Records, vol. 28, pp. 174, 175.

14 Phyllis Wheeler Grills, ed., *Kith, Kin and Cooks* (Ledyard, Connecticut: 1989), pp. 409, 422. There is no record of where Courtland went to school.

15 Ellsworth S. Grant, *The Miracle of Connecticut* (Hartford: The Connecticut Historical Society, 1992), p.245.

given in an elaborately decorated hall. Ethelinda completed rigorous training in the piano, harp, and guitar and graduated from Music Vale in 1860.

By the time young Irvin was ready for secondary school, a private academy stressing the classics and other college preparatory subjects existed in the Stonington section of Mystic Bridge. Captain John Knight Bucklyn, a Civil War veteran and Medal of Honor recipient, founded the Mystic Valley English and Classical Institute in 1868. Bucklyn had served on Major General John Sedgwick's staff with the Army of the Potomac and had been wounded at Fredericksburg and Gettysburg. The institute was housed in a large Italianate building on Lincoln Avenue, halfway between Washington Street and East Main Street. The school, which also trained students in public speaking, gymnastics, and military drill, accepted some boarders along with the day students. In 1873, enrollment included thirty female students and forty-two boys.[16] Irvin Langworthy commuted to school daily by horse and buggy from Darling Hill. He traveled the dirt track past the Samuel Langworthy farm, down the hill, across the cove by the Thomas Miner house, picking up the new (1868) road, which rounded Wilcox corner and connected "the romantic hamlet of Quiambog" with Denison Avenue and Washington Street in Mystic.[17] By the fall of 1873 Irvin was studying algebra and reading Virgil, and he hoped to go on to medical school.[18]

---

16   Carol W. Kimball, "Mystic Valley Institute," *The Day* (New London), July 10, 1986. Kimball reports that the school closed in 1906, and the building was torn down in 1918.

17   "The Quiambog Road," *Mystic Pioneer,* June 15, 1867. In 1870 Henry D. Langworthy, Samuel Langworthy, and Franklin Hancox signed an agreement with the Town of Stonington granting right of way through their lands for the portion of road (now Route 1) from Quiambog Cove eastward to the intersection with Flanders Road. They received no money for granting the right of way. Town of Stonington Land Records, vol. 40, p. 529.

18   *Hartford Daily Courant,* April 25, 1874.

Captain Bucklyn also directed the Sunday school at Mystic's Union Baptist Church, the Langworthys' church. In the 1870s, the temperance movement was at its height in the area, and Bucklyn took an active role in the Mystic Temperance Union. He also hosted biweekly meetings of the Youth's Temperance Alliance at the Mystic Valley Institute.

As STAUNCH BAPTISTS, Henry and Maria Langworthy joined in the temperance fervor and frequently attended Sunday evening temperance meetings organized jointly by a number of the churches in Mystic. However, it was precisely this predictable routine that led to the most tragic event of their lives. On Sunday, April 19, 1874, the Langworthys left the farm on Darling Hill around 5:30 p.m. and set off in their horse-drawn carriage for the Union Baptist Church to hear a sermon on the moral and philosophical aspects of temperance. Their son Courtland stayed at the farm to help the hired man finish the evening chores, and seventeen-year-old Irvin remained inside the house.

Shortly after 10 that evening, returning from Mystic, the Langworthys had just made their way up the steep hill and were passing the house where Henry's nephew Samuel Chesebrough Langworthy and his wife lived.[19] Suddenly, as they later told the story, a man came running toward them shouting something unintelligible. The night was dark, only slightly illuminated by a new crescent moon low in the western sky, and rain clouds were gathering as a nor'easter brewed. Not recognizing the fellow or understanding what he was saying, Henry drove the eighth of a

---

19   Henry's brother Samuel Langworthy Jr. died in 1872 and left his son Samuel Chesebrough Langworthy his house on the (Lord's) hill. His widow, Prudence, continued to live there also until she died in 1881. In 1867, the younger Samuel married Sarah C. Hancox, daughter of Captain Franklin Hancox, who lived down the hill on Wamphassuc Road.

mile on to his own farmyard. As he was leading his horse into the carriage house, Henry was followed by the disheveled man, who turned out to be his own hired farm hand, Bill Libby. Libby was blurting out a story about two men entering the house, striking him on the head, and killing Irvin. Upon delivering this shocking news, Libby complained of a bleeding head wound and retreated into the stable "to lie down and die."

Maria and Henry, shaken but not knowing what to think, quickly covered the few steps to the house. Entering the kitchen by the west door, Henry groped about in the darkness and soon put his hand on his youngest son, Irvin, still sitting in a chair next to the kitchen table. His head was thrown back, and his feet remained propped up on the sofa. Libby had told the truth. The boy was dead. According to newspaper accounts, Maria, standing in the doorway, began to faint, and Henry rushed her back to his nephew Samuel's house.

Shortly, Henry returned to the Darling Hill farm with his nephew Samuel and several other men to investigate the situation. The lamp on the table next to Irvin's chair had been tipped over and broken into a thousand pieces. The book Irvin had been reading, some later said a religious tract, had fallen on the floor. An, article in the *Stonington Mirror* later described the scene with an almost poetic Gothic precision. Seventeen-year-old Irvin's face "was calm and placid in its expression, not a mark upon it, not a feature distorted; but on the head, exactly in the centre of the crown, was a gaping ghastly wound, from which the blood trickled in a fast congealing pool on the floor beneath."

"The boy had died as he sat, without the movement of a muscle," the article continued. "There were no evidences of a struggle; there was not a drop of blood upon the walls nor floor, save where it had dripped directly beneath the chair."[20] Even the loose strips of carpeting on the floor were undisturbed.

The men then became concerned about Irvin's older brother Courtland, and they started for the back stairway that led to his room above the kitchen. Again, the *Stonington Mirror*'s description was vivid: "Here the sickening evidences of the murderer's presence were first revealed in the tracks he had left behind him. The walls of the narrow stairway and little passage above were splashed with blood, and great clots and smears upon the corners showed where the assassin had laid his hand." In his small room, the 33-year-old Courtland lay "face downward upon the bed…insensible from a great gash at the base of his skull, but breathing heavily. The place looked a shambles, the pillows were nothing but a clot of gore, and even the mattresses beneath were saturated through and through. The floor under the bed was slippery, and a great pool had formed in one corner with the flow."[21] Courtland had evidently been struck while he was asleep, and although he had lost much blood his skull had not been fractured, and he was still alive.

Samuel Langworthy immediately sent a rider down to Stonington Borough to fetch Dr. Charles Brayton and Constable Samuel Tillinghast. The two men reached Darling Hill close to midnight. The 23-year-old Dr. Brayton, who had just taken over Dr. William Hyde's practice after graduating from Columbia College Medical School the spring before, did his best to minister to Courtland and dress his wound.[22] He also was called upon to lay out Irvin's body.

---

20   *Stonington Mirror*, April 23, 1874.
21   Ibid.
22   *Biographical Review of New London County, Connecticut,* vol. 36 (Boston: Biographical Review Publishing Co., 1898), p. 51.

18 • Mystery and Rumors

Meanwhile, Tillinghast, one of five constables in the town, surveyed the scene and searched the premises for evidence, such as a murder weapon. A four-foot oak shaft, actually a whiffle-tree used to attach horses' harnesses to a wagon, was discovered behind the stove in the kitchen, but the stains on it were old. The search continued in the farm's several outbuildings. An axe, with hair and bloodstains on its head, was discovered in the woodshed, and a three-foot-long iron drill was eventually found in the barn. The drill also had blood on it. A shotgun, left standing in the carriage house, caused some consternation, but its stock was clean, and it was determined that the boys' wounds were too deep to have been made by a gunstock.

Henry Langworthy and the other men at the farm that night were aware that the hired man, Libby, was in the stable lying on the floor apparently suffering from head wounds. Constable Tillinghast went to the stable to question the man and became suspicious when Libby's account of the evening's events yielded contradictions. Furthermore, "when taken, much against his will, into the presence of the dead young man, [Libby was] said to have perspired like a man mowing, and this was interpreted as a sign of guilt."[23]

Tillinghast was familiar with bloodshed. A second lieutenant in the 26th Regiment of Connecticut Volunteers in the Civil War, he had himself been wounded eleven years earlier at the battle of Port Hudson in Louisiana.[24] Confident that he had enough

---

23 *Mystic Press*, April 24, 1874.

24 *History of New London County*, p. 820. The soldiers in Company H of Connecticut's 26th Regiment were recruited largely from the Stonington area. Ten members were wounded and one died at Port Hudson, Louisiana, on May 27, 1863. A memorial to the Battle of Port Hudson is situated on the southeast side of the Civil War monument in front of the Mystic Congregational Church. In 1874, Samuel K. Tillinghast lived at 10 Harmony Street in the Borough.

evidence, he proceeded to arrest Libby on the spot. Sometime after midnight, Tillinghast escorted Libby down to the Borough and put him in a cell in the lock-up on Church Street. The *Mystic Press* reported that "little sleep was had in the Harbor or Quiambog districts during the night."[25]

Early Monday morning, Justice of the Peace William R. Palmer summoned an inquest jury made up of a cross-section of Borough men to determine the cause of Irvin's death. Palmer, who had served in 8th Connecticut Regiment in the Civil War, owned a dry goods store on the northwest corner of Water and Grand Streets. Edward C. Denison, the jury's foreman, had been a village constable, tax collector, and grand juror. He was the agent for the Providence and Stonington Steamship Co. for twenty-four years and lived on Grand Street. The clerk of the jury was Stiles Stanton, a resident of Main Street. This distinguished 70-year-old probate judge had been an incorporator of the now-dissolved Stonington Savings Bank and a director of the Borough's Ocean Bank. Other jurors included Captain William Brewster, the lawyer Edwin B. Trumbull, and a hardware store owner, Erastus Chesebro, who owned land in the southeast part of the village and was the chief engineer of the Neptune Fire Engine Company, the Borough's only fire company at the time. Local men of humbler positions filled the remaining seats: the grocer Edward Sheffield; a twenty-six-year-old clerk, Edward P. Teed; a carpenter, Charles Greenman; a shoemaker, Charles Moore; a teamster, Thomas Hinckley; and Albert Gates.[26]

The northeast storm brought heavy rain Monday morning. Nevertheless, members of the inquest jury abandoned their

---

25 *Mystic Press,* April 24, 1874.
26 *Stonington Mirror,* April 23, 1874. *Anderson's 1881 Stonington Directory* (Stonington, Connecticut: J.A. Anderson, 1881).

usual routines and made their way in horse-drawn carriages up to Farmer's Palace on Darling Hill, arriving around 11 a.m. However, when they entered the kitchen, all traces of the previous night's horror had been scrubbed away by some of Maria Langworthy's well-meaning neighbors, and Irvin's body was neatly laid out in another room. All they could do was to examine the gash in the boy's head. The back stairway and Courtland's room had not been touched, so they were able to view that scene. Courtland, who had always been a rather weak boy and was practically blind, was hovering between life and death. In consideration of his limitations and the fact that he had undoubtedly been struck while asleep, there was almost no possibility of learning anything from him. The inquest jurors returned to the village.

The jury reconvened at two o'clock on Monday afternoon in a "closed-door session" at the Borough Hall on Church Street.[27] The first order of business was to interrogate the only witness, the prisoner. Earlier that morning at the lock-up, Constable Tillinghast had encountered a New London lawyer, Oscar Hewitt, and John A. Tibbits, editor of the *New London Evening Telegram*, interviewing Libby as he lay on his bunk.[28] Roused out of his cell, Libby entered the room, his head wrapped with a stained

---

27   The Stonington Borough Hall with the lock-up was situated on Church Street opposite the present Borough Hall, and was torn down in 1900. Williams Haynes, *Stonington Chronology*. (Stonington, Connecticut: Pequot Press, 1949) p. 91.

28   Oscar Hewitt was a lawyer and judge of the New London Police Court. He lived at 156 Bank Street and had an office at 19 1/2 Bank Street. He wrote the police court column in the *New London Evening Telegram*, often in verse and limericks. John A. Tibbits (1844-1893) was a major in the Army in the Civil War and was wounded at Antietam; he was the editor of the *Evening Telegram* from 1873 to 1881 and became the first editor and publisher of the New London *Day (1881)*. The *New London Evening Telegram* offices were on Green Street; *New London Directory* (New London: Andrew Boyd, 1875). *New London Evening Telegram*, January 22, 1875.

handkerchief and "his hair somewhat clotted with blood from the wound which he had received, as he asserts, from the men who killed Irvin."[29]

A powerfully built man with brown hair and a ruddy complexion, Libby stood almost six feet tall and must have weighed close to 200 pounds. The *Stonington Mirror* bluntly described his face as "not a bad one, though by no means intelligent." He was wearing an "old ragged suit of clothes" and a "round visorless cap such as is worn by seamen in the navy, his appearance altogether that of a man who had led a hard kind of life."[30] As for his wounds, they did not seem, according to the account, to be at all serious and could even have been self-inflicted. In response to questions from the jury, he spoke in a calm and straightforward manner.

The witness stated his full name, William B. Libby, and that he had been born in Lewiston, Maine, where his father owned a farm. He said he was twenty-two years old, although reporters guessed that he was about thirty. Three years earlier, he said, he had enlisted in the Navy and, after serving on "several vessels," ended up on the *Canandaigua*, a sloop with an illustrious record for the Union side in the Civil War. It was still in service cruising the Caribbean.[31] In September 1873, his term of enlistment was up. Libby said he was honorably discharged in Philadelphia and then traveled to New York City, where, on his first day, he was robbed of all his money. He immediately decided to head toward New England and took the night

---

29 *New London Evening Telegram*, April 20, 1874.
30 *Stonington Mirror*, April 23, 1874.
31 The *Canandaigua*, launched in Boston in 1862, was part of the South Atlantic Blockading Squadron off Charleston, South Carolina. On February 17, 1864, she rescued 150 crew members of the *Housatonic*, which had been attacked by the Confederate submarine *H. L. Hunley*. The *Canandaigua* was finally decommissioned in November 1875. www.data.historycentral.com/navy.

boat to Stonington. (Apparently, he was not robbed of "all" of his money, or found some other way to obtain money for the passage.)

Arriving at the Stonington steamboat dock in the morning, he walked over to Water Street and began to inquire about work. Before long, he met up with Henry Langworthy, who was standing outside Henry Stanton's store on Water Street. The Langworthys owned the adjacent building (just south of Stanton's on the east side of Water between the railroad right of way and Grand Street), and they leased it to Edward Sheffield for his grocery store.[32] Libby struck an agreement with Langworthy, and he told the jurors that he had been working at the Darling Hill farm for the previous six months. When asked whether he had had any "difficulty" with either Irvin or Courtland, Libby replied that he had not.

The inquest jury then wanted to hear Libby's version of what had happened on the previous evening. In response to questions from Trumbull, he testified that after Mr. and Mrs. Langworthy left for Mystic, he finished the evening's chores, with some help from Courtland. They then went inside and ate supper with Irvin. Once the dishes were cleared, Irvin got his book and sat down at the table with his back to the door. Libby picked up Friday's *Norwich Advertiser* and sat down at the table to smoke, about three feet from Irvin, also with his back to the door. Courtland played with the dog for a bit, but soon decided to go to bed. He was barefoot and went upstairs about 8:30 without taking a lamp. Libby said that he had talked with Irvin and read. Suddenly, without noise or warning, "a long light colored bar or

---

32   Lucy Rodman sold 139 (now 141) Water St. to Maria P. Langworthy on March 15, 1864. Town of Stonington Land Records vol. 29, p. 404. Note that, since 1809, married women in Connecticut could own property in their own names. Stanton's store is now 143 Water Street.

club pushed by his head and fell on Irvin." The lamp went crashing over, and a blow to his own head knocked him to the floor. Two more blows "rendered him insensible."

Although Libby had told Samuel Langworthy and others the night before that two men had entered the house by the east door, delivered blows to Irvin and himself, and that he had "fought them off," he told the jury that "he heard no one before the blow was struck and did not see two men in the house."[33] When the Langworthy kitchen was searched, a copy of the *Norwich Advertiser* had not been found on or near the table.[34] In fact, the Friday paper turned up "at the bottom of quite a number of papers in a rack which hung upon the wall."[35] No one remembered putting the paper away, thus another possible discrepancy in Libby's story.

The jury then heard from Henry Langworthy. He swore that Libby told him on Sunday night that he had been attacked by two men. Langworthy also testified that Libby was a "good natured, obedient man," and that he was not aware of any difficulty between his boys and the hired man. Langworthy did have one fault to find with Libby, and that was his "liability to get drunk" on cider, not a very surprising remark from a temperance man.[36] More witnesses were questioned—Constable Tillinghast, Dr. Brayton, Samuel C. Langworthy, William Perkins, and Harry F. Chesebro—but little new information was uncovered.

Both Constable Tillinghast and Samuel Langworthy swore that Libby had mentioned two men, one in a light coat. Another

---

33 *Stonington Mirror*, April 23, 1874.

34 The *Norwich Advertiser* was the only local Democratic newspaper during this period. The *Advertiser* suspended publication in August 1874.

35 *New London Evening Telegram*, April 21, 1874.

36 *Stonington Mirror*, April 23, 1874.

witness, Thomas Colbert, was able to shed some light on this puzzling part of the investigation. Colbert, an engineer on the Shore Line railroad, according to the *New London Evening Telegram*, was returning in a carriage from Mystic about 9 o'clock. "Between the houses of Samuel and Henry Langworthy," the account continued, "two men jumped out into the road and crossed it, frightening the horse and causing him to shy. Colbert got out to lead the horse back into the road, and his attention was called to the fact that one of the men wore a light coat. Since then, it's been established that they are friends of Colbert, who had secreted themselves alongside the road just for the purpose of giving him a scare."[37] Actually, the two appear to have been Samuel Langworthy's trusted farm hands. Libby had mentioned the "man in a light coat" story to Tibbits on Monday morning, but then dropped the story altogether when he testified. The inquest jury agreed to adjourn until Saturday, April 25.

ON TUESDAY, APRIL 21, Dr. Brayton, assisted by the medical examiner, Dr. George D. Stanton, performed a post mortem on the body of Irvin Langworthy.[38] Meanwhile, in the Borough, William Libby was brought before Justice of the Peace William R. Palmer and charged with Irvin's murder as well as assault with the intent to kill Courtland Langworthy. Libby pleaded not guilty to both charges. No bail was permitted in a murder case, and he certainly was unable to provide the $10,000 bail for the charge of assault. Palmer officially "bound the prisoner over for trial at the next term of the Superior Court for New London County." Late in the day, Deputy Sheriff Frank M. Clemence escorted Libby to New London, where he was "lodged in jail."

---

37 *New London Evening Telegram*, April 20, 1874.
38 George Dallas Stanton (1839-1916) graduated from Bellevue Hospital Medical College in 1865. Grills, *Kith, Kin and Cooks*, p. 355.

The *New London Evening Telegram* noted that he was "without friends or family here...or money to retain counsel."[39]

NEW LONDON COUNTY Sheriff O. N. Raymond and his deputy appeared at the Darling Hill farm on Wednesday morning to examine the premises and question the elder Langworthys. Although Maria was preparing the house for her son's funeral that afternoon, she tried to remember details and respond. As for the recovering Courtland, "while the officers were conversing with his parents, he would occasionally interrupt the conversation with 'Bill knows all about it,' but could give no reasons."[40] Earlier in the week, the *New London Evening Telegram* divulged that Courtland was not only weak and nearly blind, but that

First New York Times story on murder, April 21, 1874

---

39 *New London Evening Telegram*, April 22, 1874.
40 Ibid., April 23, 1874.

he was "decidedly non compos mentis."[41] Jerome S. Anderson, editor of the *Stonington Mirror*[42], and L. M. Guernsey[43] of the *Mystic Press* must have felt constrained to hold back this information regarding the son of one of the town's leading citizens.

After thoroughly examining the various possible murder weapons at the farm, the officers were of the opinion that both sons' wounds had been inflicted with the three-foot "steel drill, octagonal in shape and tapering off to a point at one end," that had been found in the barn.[44] The drill, which was used to break up boulders, did have fresh blood stains on it, but whether they were human still had to be determined. The sheriff concluded that owing to the isolated location and complex layout of the farm, the crimes could only have been committed by someone "well acquainted with the premises as it would have been impossible for a stranger to find his way."[45]

IRVIN LANGWORTHY'S FUNERAL was held at 2 on Wednesday afternoon inside Farmer's Palace on Darling Hill. An "immense crowd" attended. "The spacious house was filled with neighbors

---

41   Ibid., April 20, 1874.

42   Jerome S. Anderson was the son of the Reverend Jerome S. Anderson, pastor of the First Baptist Church in the Borough from 1832 to 1843. He served in the Civil War with the 132nd Indiana Regiment, returned to Stonington, and began publishing the *Stonington Mirror* in 1869.

43   Lucius M. Guernsey was born in East Hartford in 1824. He established his first newspaper, the pro-abolition *North and South*, in New Britain. After the Civil war, he moved to Mystic and founded the weekly *Mystic Press* in 1873. Like Henry Langworthy, he was a member of the Union Baptist Church and was active in the temperance movement. *The Historical, Statistical and Industrial Review of the State of Connecticut* (New York: W.S. Webb & Co., 1884), Part 2, p. 306.

44   *New London Evening Telegram*, April 23, 1874.

45   Ibid.

and sympathizing friends from a distance, the yard being well filled with teams." Captain Bucklyn served as a sort of master of ceremonies, and eight of Irvin's schoolmates from the Mystic Valley Institute acted as pallbearers. The boys were members of the Young People's group at the Union Baptist Church, as Irvin had been. At the group's regular meeting on Monday evening, forty teenagers had attended, and "every one of them spoke with deep feeling of their murdered companion and brother." Others remarked that he was a "quiet and inoffensive fellow."

The coffin, placed in one of the parlors, was "most tastefully

dressed with a profusion of beautiful flowers" provided by Irvin's school, and "the face of the corpse looked peaceful and natural, giving no hint of a violent death." The Rev. G. L. Hunt of Mystic's Union Baptist Church conducted the service, assisted by both the Rev. Mr. Henry A. Wales of the Borough's Second Congregational Church and the Rev. Dr. Albert Gallatin Palmer of the Borough's First Baptist Church. A somber procession then left Darling Hill for the burial in Stonington's Evergreen Cemetery on North Main Street.[46]

ONE FAMILY MEMBER missing from the funeral was Irvin's older brother, James Hamilton Langworthy. The twenty-eight-year-old Hamilton, as he was known, had left Noank April 15, the Wednesday before the murder, aboard the *Frances A. Brooks*. This schooner smack, built in Mystic in 1868 and owned by a Noank group, was halibut fishing off the New England coast.[47] Whether Hamilton, despite holding an engineering degree, had turned to fishing for a living cannot be determined. In any event, he was in Edgartown, Massachusetts, when he read about his brother's murder

James Hamilton Langworthy

---

46   *Mystic Press*, April 24, 1874.
47   William N. Peterson, *"Mystic Built," Ships and Shipyards of the Mystic River, Connecticut, 1784-1919* (Mystic, Connecticut: Mystic Seaport Museum, Inc., 1989), p. 191.

Mystery and Rumors • 29

in a newspaper.[48] Making his way back to Stonington as quickly as possible (probably by steamship from New Bedford or Fall River), Hamilton arrived home on Friday, two days after the funeral.

ON SATURDAY AFTERNOON, April 25, the inquest jury met in the office of E. B. Trumbull, on Water Street at the corner of Railroad Avenue. Hamilton Langworthy was the first witness. He testified that, in his opinion, Libby was "a man of strong passion and very violent disposition." Irvin and Libby, he said, "had had disputes but nothing more serious than is liable to occur in any family."[49] Furthermore, he did not admit to noting any animosity between Libby and his brothers strong enough to elicit such murderous attacks. Contrary to rumors, which had been circulating around town since Tuesday and had appeared in the press as early as Wednesday, Hamilton confirmed positively that no insurance policy existed on either of his brothers' lives.

The jury then heard from Drs. Stanton and Brayton about the post mortem. They testified in painstaking detail about both boys' wounds, asserting that the cause of Irvin's death was a severe fracture of the skull. Dr. Stanton had been able to send the drill—now reported to have been found in the woodshed—to New London to be examined under a microscope by a Dr. Nelson, who "was satisfied that the stains upon it were of human blood." In Dr. Stanton's opinion, the drill was the likely murder weapon. With that, the jury took some time to deliberate and then issued a statement "to the effect that Irvin Langworthy

---

48   Nineteenth-century newspapers readily picked up stories from around the country concerning violent crimes. The Langworthy murder story was carried by papers in Hartford, New Haven, New York, and throughout New England. It may have appeared in many more papers across the country.

49   *Stonington Mirror*, April 30, 1874.

came to his death by a blow from an instrument or weapon in the hands of a person to the jury unknown."[50]

FROM THE MOMENT the news of Irvin's murder and the attempt on Courtland's life spread through the Stonington area, the crime became "wrapped in mystery," as the *New London Evening Telegram* termed it.[51] The word "mystery," frequently used in nineteenth century newspapers to characterize murders, signaled a crime so horrible and immoral that it defied explanation. This was especially true of violent murder committed in the home, a violation of the sentimentally cherished domestic space. Townsfolk immediately began to look for traces of evidence, a motive, and of course suspects. Although Libby might have been a possible suspect, no one could really find that he had any motive. As Jerome Anderson, publisher and editor of the *Stonington Mirror*, put it, "It passes human credibility that, without a spark of passion, he could deliberately murder two men with whom he had been on almost fraternal terms."[52]

If William Libby had not committed the crimes, another suspect could still be at large in the community. Alternative theories began to surface. People spoke of "an unusual number of tramps in town the day and night of the murder."[53] Tramps had committed hideous murders elsewhere, and the *Stonington Mirror* reminded readers of an atrocious slaughter in Arkansas and the Bender

---

50   Ibid.
51   *New London Evening Telegram* headline, April 20, 1874.
52   *Stonington Mirror*, April 23, 1874.
53   *Mystic Press*, April 24, 1874. A nationwide depression in 1873 created widespread unemployment, and many laid-off workers had no choice but to roam the countryside looking for farm work. The *Stonington Mirror* took note several times of the town's rising "tramp problem" in the 1870s. *Stonington Mirror*, April 23, 1874.

> **THE LANGWORTHY MURDER.**
> *Special Dispatch to the New-York Times.*
> STONINGTON, Conn., April 25.—The Coroner's jury in the Langworthy murder case met this afternoon, and after the examination of several witnesses, returned a verdict to the effect that Irving Langworthy came to his death at the hands of a person or persons to the jury unknown. Libby, the hired man, who is suspected of being connected with the murder, has been examined by a Justice of the Peace, and held to appear at the next term of the Superior Court. A town meeting has been called for next week, to offer a reward for the apprehension of the murderer, and to request the State authorities to do the same.

From the New York Times, April 25, 1874

murders in Kansas, both widely reported at the time. But any sort of robbery had been ruled out. Nothing had been stolen. Two secretary desks in the Langworthy house, where money might have been kept, were untouched. Anderson put into words the apprehension and growing frustration of his readers: "The need of an experienced detective is sorely felt, and the delay of town officers in not ordering one immediately is severely criticized."[54]

The climate of mystery that "enveloped the case" quickly bred rumors and innuendo. As early as the evening following the attacks, the *New London Evening Telegram* stated, "Some rumors of a startling and horrible nature calculated to throw suspicion upon others than Libby are whispered about, but their publication at this time could accomplish no good end and might cast an unjust

---

54 *Stonington Mirror*, April 23, 1874.

imputation upon those who are entirely innocent of any participation in the foul deed."⁵⁵

One matter that aroused suspicion was that of the insurance policies, and two days later, the *Telegram* did address the issue. Despite stating that it "would not mention it," the paper could not resist reporting that "absurd" rumors had "become public property not only in Stonington, but throughout this section of the county." The implication was that, if Henry Langworthy had had insurance policies on his sons' lives, perhaps he had a powerful motive to mastermind the horrible crime. However, the *Telegram* maintained that Langworthy was "worthy and respectable." He owned a "handsome farm property and sufficient of this world's goods." Why would he have taken out policies on the "weak" Courtland or, for that matter, Irvin, who was "deformed"? (Evidently, Irvin had "but one ear," although he seems to have been normal in every other respect.) To put the matter to rest—"to remove the unjust and awful suspicions that have been whispered about"—the *Telegram* had written to Henry Langworthy asking if he carried life insurance on his boys, and if so, who was the beneficiary. Since it was thought that Langworthy "set considerable store by the 'almighty dollar,'" the editors had enclosed a 3-cent postage stamp to insure his reply. ⁵⁶

On Saturday, April 25, the same day the inquest jury issued its verdict of murder, the suspicions and rumors exploded from local town gossip into a national arena. Forces implicating Henry Langworthy found a newspaper outside the local area that would publish their story without any qualms. The headline in the Saturday *New York Times* read, "THE STONINGTON MURDER, A New Aspect Put on the Tragedy, Some History of the

---

55   *New London Evening Telegram*, April 20, 1874.
56   Ibid., April 22, 27, 1874.

THE STONINGTON MURDER.

A NEW ASPECT PUT ON THE TRAGEDY.

SOME HISTORY OF THE LANGWORTHY FAMILY—THE MOTIVE FOR THE MURDER.

From Our Own Correspondent.

STONINGTON, Wednesday, April 22, 1874

There is no new development of facts in the Langworthy tragedy as yet, but as the rumors to which I alluded in my last dispatch have become matters of public discussion, there need be no hesitation now in giving them further publicity, and for this purpose some description of the Langworthy family may be needed. Henry D. Langworthy, the father of the murdered boy, is a man sixty or sixty-five years old, who was born in this vicinity, and who for many years has owned and conducted a dairy farm a mile west of the village of Stonington. He is what is called in the vernacular a "well-to-do" man, and is even reputed wealthy. His business transactions have always been marked by the greatest shrewdness, and he has the name of being an extremely avaricious man, with whom the desire for gain commonly outweighs any scruples of conscience. He has always occupied a respectable position in society, however, notwithstanding some very dubious transactions in the past, which are now being restored to light. He married his first cousin in early life, and had several children by her, all of whom, with one exception, were marked with the physical and mental defects which are the inheritance of offspring of a consanguineous marriage. The boy Irving who was killed had only one ear; Cortland, the eldest son, who was left for dead, was nearly blind, and little better than an idiot; a daughter, who died some years ago, was also nearly blind, and all showed the evidences of feeble intellects and ill-balanced minds. Mrs. Langworthy is said to be a woman of considerable culture and refinement, but those who know her best say, rather indefinitely, that she is queer, and certainly her conduct in the past has been at least eccentric. A short time before the death of the daughter she united with her husband in forcing her into a marriage with a disreputable character here, to whom they gave $700 and a piano as an inducement to make her his wife. He treated her most brutally, and in a short time they instituted a suit against him for divorce and alimony. The girl was opposed to the proceeding, but they obliged her to unite with them, and they won the suit. The evidence offered on the trial was disgusting beyond description, and the case stands on record as pre-eminently the most revolting one ever tried in this county. Shortly after its conclusion the girl, who was a feeble, sickly person, died, as it was generally believed, from the shock of the horrible exposure she was obliged to make, and the father sued the husband for the amount of the attending physician's bill. There were then left in the family only the three sons, Hamilton, who at the time of the murder was at sea, and Cortland and Irving, the young men who were assai[led].

On the morning after the murder, which I be remembered, was discovered not long before ...night Sunday, Langworthy, the father, was around the village as usual serving his customers with milk. He appeared in no wise overcome by the terrible tragedy, and while the jury of inquest was examining the body of his son he showed no emotion whatever. Had he been an indifferent person he could not have retained his self-composure more thoroughly. This conduct was generally noticed and was severely commented upon. Last night a relative of the family is said to have stated that the father held life insurance policies on each of his sons to the amount of $10,000. This is corroborated by a gentleman who was told a few months ago by the agent of a New-York company that he had visited the Langworthy family and taken a total risk of $50,000 on the five members. These were facts which at once set the village quidnuncs to speculating, and some very ugly stories are afloat today, strongly corroborated by circumstances, which I am not at liberty to mention. The authorities have telegraphed to various insurance companies and agencies, but thus far have received no response. Now, the great mystery which envelopes the murder arises wholly from the utter absence of any motive. Libbey, the hired man, who is now held on suspicion, tells a very confused story. At the time of his arrest he informed the officer that he was attacked by two men, and that before he saw them he heard a dog bark outside, heard a step behind him, and then received a blow which rendered him insensible. But in his statement before the jury of inquest he denied this, saying that he saw a club fall on Irving's head, and almost on the instant was knocked out of his chair and struck twice while he lay upon the floor; that he saw no one, and heard no one. But his wounds are very slight. In the opinion of medical men, they were insufficient to produce insensibility, and in view of this and the facts that there was a dog about the house trained to bark at strangers; that the handles of the door are loose, and cannot be turned without considerable noise, and that in the position in which Irving and Libbey sat it was necessary for any one approaching from behind to strike over the latter's head to inflict a fatal blow—in view of all these circumstances, his story is received with doubt, though otherwise it is plausible enough. But if it be true, and the murder was the work of tramps or professional thieves, why was there nothing of value taken from the house? Why was the boy, from whom little resistance could be expected, attacked before the powerful man? Why, too, was an assault made on an unoffending man asleep on the floor above—a man who knew nothing of what was in progress below, and who, being nearly blind, could never have accused nor identified the thieves? These are questions which cannot be reasonably answered.

But on the other hand, what incentive had Libbey to the commission of the crime? It has been shown that there was no ill-feeling between him and the boys; the brother, who is now recovering from his wounds, confirms this. The appearance of the room in which the murder was committed; the posture of the body; the nature of the wound, all preclude the idea of a struggle that evening. There was not a mark or bruise upon the boy save the gaping wound in the head behind and the fracture of the skull, reaching nearly from forehead to base. Everything goes to show that the boy was sitting quietly in his chair reading when he was struck, and died as he sat, almost without the movement of a muscle. His elbow was upon the table where he was found; his book lay at his feet. The blow was from above and behind, and it was given without warning. There was no blood in the room except immediately beneath the chair; had there been an encounter, or had the boy fallen to the floor when he was struck, and subsequently been replaced as he was found, the effusion was so profuse and sudden that the floor must have been stained where he laid. It is impossible to believe that he moved after that crushing blow; one must believe that as he was found so he died. And accepting this, one cannot overcome the conviction that it was a cold-blooded, deliberately-planned murder. And this is confirmed by the circumstances of the attack upon Cortlandt. No sudden gust of passion could have sent a man through the long halls and passages leading to his room to murder one he had not seen for at least two hours. The murder was preconceived with atrocious perfection of detail and was executed with the same cold-blooded deliberation.

Public reasoning here takes this position: If Libbey committed the murder he was actuated by one of two motives—enmity to the young men or the expectation of profiting by their death. The first hypothesis is rejected utterly for the reasons given above. The other, with its terrible possibilities, remains unanswered. Was Libbey hired to do this crime, and, if so, by whom? And if the above reasoning is correct it applies equally to any other person, supposing Libbey to be innocent.

There is a thoroughly good officer here, S. K. Tillinghast, who is working up the case, and it is hoped that when the jury of inquest meets next Saturday some conclusive evidence will be brought before it. Until that time no new developments will be made known. But, in the meantime, the current of public suspicion, not to say opinion, is very strongly marked, even more strongly than is indicated by what I have said above.

Tillinghast

From the New York Times, April 25, 1874

Langworthy Family—The Motive for the Murder."[57] The story had been filed "from Our Own Correspondent" on Wednesday, April 22. This unidentified reporter had written the initial story of the murder earlier in the week for the *Times*[58] and was now ready to give some of the rumors "further publicity." Clearly, the writer was well acquainted with the Langworthys and felt no reservations about casting suspicion on them. The *Times*'s correspondent began his article by characterizing Henry D. Langworthy as a "well-to-do" man. In fact, Langworthy's 1874 property assessment did amount to $11,379, making him one of the fifty wealthiest people in Stonington at the time. (However, his assessment did not approach that of Charles P. Williams at $815,000, or Sarah Stone McEckron at $220,000, or even Richard F. Loper at $86,000.[59]) While Langworthy was a "shrewd" businessman, the writer maintained, he also had the reputation of being "an extremely avaricious man with whom the desire for gain commonly outweighs any scruples of conscience." It is unclear exactly how Henry Langworthy earned this stinging reputation, but clearly his relative wealth did not come from farming alone. During the 1840s and 1850s, he invested in five Mystic whaling vessels and three Stonington ships. His fellow owners in these ventures included such leaders of the whaling industry as George Greenman, Charles Mallory, Elisha Faxon, and Nathaniel B. Palmer.[60]

---

57   *New York Times*, April 25, 1874.

58   "One Man Killed and Another Fatally Wounded—A Terrible Scene," *New York Times*, April 21, 1874.

59   List of Taxable Property, Town of Stonington, 1874, and *Stonington Mirror*, February 25, March 5, 1875. Sarah Stone McEckron (1864-1953) inherited the property known as Cove Lawn on North Main Street from her mother when she was a child. She married Edward F. Darrell in 1895.

60   Henry D. Langworthy is listed as part owner of the *Vermont*, the *Atlantic*, the *Robin Hood*, the *Coriolanus*, and the *Trescott*, all of Mystic, and the *Cabinet*, the *Cincinnati*, and the schooner *Flying Cloud*, all of Stonington, Connecticut. Ship Database, www.mysticseaport.org/library.

Mystery and Rumors • 35

The article went on: Langworthy "had always occupied a respectable position in society, however, notwithstanding some very dubious transactions in the past, which are now being restored to light." (No small thanks to this correspondent.) According to the writer, one of these "dubious transactions" happened to be the fact that Mr. and Mrs. Langworthy had a "consanguineous marriage"–they were first cousins. This union had resulted in children with "physical and mental defects." Courtland was "little better than an idiot," and their daughter was also "nearly blind" and possessed an "ill-balanced mind." Irvin was missing one ear. No mention was made of the bright and handsome Hamilton.

Maria Langworthy then came in for the same back-of-the-hand treatment by the *Times* correspondent. While she was "said to be a woman of considerable culture and refinement," those who knew Mrs. Langworthy "best" said she was "queer," and her past conduct had been "at least eccentric." At this point, the writer's defamatory story did provide some facts. Apparently, back in 1866, Maria and Henry Langworthy, concerned that their twenty-five-year-old daughter Ethelinda was still single, had arranged for her to marry Henry C. Stanton, their twenty-eight-year-old neighboring shopkeeper on Water Street. The *New York Times* reporter described it this way: Maria "united with her husband in forcing her [daughter] into a marriage with a disreputable character here, to whom they gave $700 and a piano as an inducement to make her his wife."

The story that followed bears retelling, despite the sensational hyperbole. Stanton "treated [Ethelinda] most brutally, and in a short time [the Langworthys] instituted a suit against him for divorce and alimony. The girl was opposed to the proceeding, but they obliged her to unite with them, and they won the suit. The evidence offered in the trial was disgusting beyond description, and the case stands on record as pre-eminently the most revolting one ever tried in this county. Shortly after its conclusion the girl, who was a feeble, sickly person, died, as it was generally believed, from the shock of the horrible exposure she was obliged to make, and the father sued the husband for the amount of the attending physician's bill."[61]

Maria Langworthy's actual role in this sordid story is obscured. But a certain amount of the *Times*'s revelation can be verified. Stonington's Registration of Marriages shows that on December 17, 1866, Henry Clay Stanton married Ethelinda Langworthy at the Second Congregational Church on Main Street in the Borough. Stanton, born in Vineyard Haven, Massachusetts, in 1838, was the second son of Captain Samuel G. Stanton and Mary Jane Hillman Stanton.[62] Although Ethelinda was twenty-five, the marriage document registered her as twenty-two.

Stanton might well have been characterized as a "disreputable character." An April 1866 diary entry by Dr. David Hart described him as "a keeper of a low groggery, [who] sold the liquor [rum], adulterated with various ingredients."[63] The Langworthys,

---

61   *New York Times*, April 25, 1874.

62   William A. Stanton, *Thomas Stanton of Connecticut and His Descendants*, (Albany, New York: Joel Munsell's Sons, 1891),p. 512. Mary Jane Hillman was from Vineyard Haven, Massachusetts. Samuel G. Stanton was born in Stonington in 1804 and died in 1882. He lived on the corner of Main and Temple streets, and his son Henry operated a livery stable in the back of the property, as well as the "saloon" on Water Street. See 1868 Beers map of Stonington Borough. In late 1869, Stanton's saloon was raided by Deputy Sheriff Raymond, and Henry Stanton was tried in April 1870 for "adulterating liquor." As a result, the 1881 Directory lists the 143 Water Street store as Stanton's Confectioners and Fruit Dealers.

63   Henry R. Palmer, Jr., ed., "The Arsonists"(diary of David S. Hart), *Historical Footnotes*, 14 (August 1977). Henry C. Stanton stored barrels of rum in the livery barn behind his father's house. In April 1866, the barn was burned down by arsonists hired by Palmer Loper, son of Richard F. Loper. Hart was acquainted with H. C. Stanton; his office was on the opposite side of Water Street and just a few doors north of the saloon.

who owned the building next to Stanton's saloon, undoubtedly knew him well. In fact, Maria Langworthy even held the mortgage on Stanton's building in 1864.[64] Henry and Maria Langworthy must have been quite anxious to have Ethelinda married, anxious enough to overlook Stanton's reputation as well as their aversion to hard liquor.

On May 15, 1867, only five months after the ill-fated marriage, Ethelinda petitioned the superior court in Norwich for a divorce from Henry Stanton. The attorneys Thomas M. Waller and Richard P. Huntley represented her, Waller being paid $50 for his services.[65] The petition stated that shortly after the marriage, "the Respondent [Stanton] became intolerably cruel towards your petitioner, continually treating [her] in such brutal and shocking manner that she became seriously ill from the effect of said brutality, and notwithstanding her illness, [this phrase was crossed out] her protestations and the persuasions of her mother, he continued in secret his said brutality from thence to the time when [he] deserted your petitioner." The petitioner Ethelinda Stanton further averred that "the Respondent has been guilty of such other misconduct as permanently destroys her happiness and defeats the purposes of the marriage relation."

In requesting a divorce along with alimony, the petitioner estimated that Stanton was "a man of comfortable means," worth from four to five thousand dollars. The sheriff was directed to attach one thousand dollars' worth of Henry Stanton's goods.

---

64 Town of Stonington Land Records, vol. 32, pp. 426, 427. Samuel G. Stanton actually owned the building, and Maria Langworthy held the mortgage in 1864, assigning it to his son Henry in December 1864.

65 Thomas M. Waller (1839-1924) was elected to the Connecticut House of Representatives in 1867. At the time of the Langworthy murder, he was mayor of New London. He went on to become speaker of the House in 1876 and governor from 1883 to 1885, among other positions that he held.

However, papers and a summons had to be delivered to Henry D. Langworthy, who retained possession of Stanton's belongings at Farmer's Palace, where the young couple had lived during their brief marriage. On May 18, Deputy Sheriff D. H. Chappell left the writ and process at the farm on Darling Hill.[66]

In September, Ethelinda's petition was granted, although the judge cited misconduct as grounds and "not because the respondent had communicated to her the disease which she claimed." He also found Stanton worth only $1,500 and awarded Ethelinda $200 in alimony to be paid by November.[67] Ethelinda was not going to be able to reap much benefit from the alimony award, but the amount might have been used to pay her doctor. By November, she was hopelessly ill with consumption, and she died on a cold, windy, snowy November 11, 1867. According to her gravestone, her dying words were, "Come blessed Saviour, come blessed Saviour. Take Etha home. He is very near."[68]

The facts of Ethelinda's pathetic marriage and death tell a story slightly different from that in the *New York Times*, one without all the cruel insinuations against Henry and Maria Langworthy. Furthermore, Ethelinda's piano was never given away. It always remained at Farmer's Palace. Regardless of how odd or "eccentric" Maria Langworthy might have been, or what her responsibility might have been in arranging her daughter's marriage, she surely must have felt remorse and grief over the outcome.

After raising doubt about Maria's character, the *New York Times* correspondent turned his attention back to Henry Langworthy.

---

66 New London County Superior Court, Divorces 1719-1875, Connecticut State Library, Record Group 3, box 33, docket #900.

67 Ibid. See letter from James Phelps, October 7, 1867.

68 Stonington Vital Records. *Mystic Pioneer*, November 16, 1867. Langworthy family plot, Evergreen (Stonington) Cemetery.

Mystery and Rumors • 39

The sixty-four-year-old father of one critically injured and one slain boy had apparently delivered milk to his customers in the Borough on Monday morning, only hours after the attacks. "He appeared in no wise overcome by the terrible tragedy." The *New London Evening Telegram* frowned on Henry's behavior as well, calling it "incredible that a father would expose himself to the eyes of the public when one son lay dead and the other supposed to be dying unless absolutely necessary for him to do so."[69] The more sympathetic *Mystic Press* had also noticed Henry out on his routine rounds on Monday but reported that he had been

---

69   *New London Evening Telegram*, April 27, 1874.

urged by friends "to go his usual route, as a means of getting his mind, which was evidently suffering from the strain, off from the distressing circumstances of his home." The *Mystic Press* reporter perhaps revealed a closer understanding of Henry's character. "As he is a man who does not stop to ask what people will say, when he chooses to do a thing, he went as advised."[70]

The gossipy rumors about insurance policies were also repeated and exaggerated in the *New York Times*. That Henry carried policies of $10,000 on each son was said to be "corroborated by a gentleman who was told a few months ago by the agent of a New York company that he had visited the Langworthy family and taken a total risk of $50,000 on the five [family] members." Just for good measure, the writer threw in the following vague but ominous statement. "Some very ugly stories are afloat today, strongly corroborated by circumstances, which I am not at liberty to mention." However, during the following week, the insurance matter would be cleared up once and for all. One of the papers had contacted The Phoenix Insurance Co. of Hartford, and the company stated that the boys were not insured by them, and that Hamilton had carried an endowment plan policy but had given it up a year earlier. Mr. and Mrs. Langworthy had life insurance policies of $5,000 each.[71] The lawyer Oscar Hewitt of New London also confirmed, in a letter to the *New Haven Register* on April 27, that the boys' "lives were not assured and their heirship could not have been an inducement."[72]

---

70   *Mystic Press*, April 24, 1874.

71   *New London Evening Telegram*, April 27, 1874. The Phoenix Mutual Insurance Company was founded in 1851 as American Temperance "selling policies to teetotalers at 25% lower premiums." By 1861, owing to slow sales, the company changed to a regular life insurance company under the name of Phoenix. E.S. Grant, *The Miracle of Connecticut*, p. 69. This explains why the Langworthys might have been partial to The Phoenix Company.

72   *Mystic Press*, May 1, 1874.

So, if the hired man Libby committed the attacks, "What incentive had [he] to the commission of the crime?" The *New York Times* reviewed the circumstances. Libby's story seemed dubious, owing in no small way to the insufficiency of his own head wounds. New details were also surfacing to poke holes in Libby's testimony. The Langworthy family dog usually barked at strangers, but no barking had been heard that night. The doorknobs in the old house were "loose" and could not be turned "without considerable noise." Libby claimed that he had heard nothing before being clubbed on the head. In the *Times*, all the evidence added up to "a cold-blooded, deliberately-planned murder," especially in view of the attack on Courtland. "No sudden gust of passion could have sent a man through the long halls and passages leading to his room to murder one he had not seen for at least two hours. The murder was preconceived with atrocious perfection of detail." Since "enmity" between Libby and the boys had not yet been proved, the motivation, in the mind of the reporter, boiled down to "the expectation of profiting by their death." Readers were finally left with this question to mull over, "Was Libby hired to do the crime, and, if so, by whom?"[73]

Stonington Mirror publisher and editor Jerome S. Anderson was troubled by the suggestive insinuations, mostly from newspapers outside the local area. Because the April 23 edition of his weekly journal had sold out, he reprinted the entire Langworthy Tragedy story from the previous week in the April 30 edition. However, he prefaced the reprint with what amounted to a powerful editorial. The "reckless" publication of these stories in the daily press, he stated, "may not be libelous, but it is to say the least ungenerous and unkind." In fact, in his opinion, the dailies were "scandal mongering on a large scale." "An honorable journalist"–perhaps himself, he seemed to suggest–"might well shrink from it."

---

73 *New York Times*, April 25, 1874.

Anderson was somewhat trapped in this situation between his journalistic duty to present the alarming story and his desire to protect his community and his friends. Nineteenth-century journalists routinely printed sensational accounts of murders in order to feed the public excitement. They also routinely claimed the moral high ground by decrying the practice. Anderson, wrestling with this dilemma, shrank from defaming his fellow Stonington citizens. "It is a grave thing to bring a charge of complicity in murder against a man." The specifics of such a charge could do irreparable injury, even after the person was cleared of the crime. If Anderson was worried about Henry Langworthy's reputation, he did not say so. He did consider "absurd and reckless" a veiled charge that Henry C. Stanton might have been the culprit.[74]

"STONINGTON IN A BAD WAY" read the headline in the next week's issue of the *Stonington Mirror*. It seems that some of the village's leading–and "wealthiest"–citizens were ready to instigate a new investigation of the murder themselves. Apparently, they were not convinced that Libby was the most likely suspect. The group circulated a petition, mostly around the Borough, calling for a town meeting to approve putting up a reward to find Irvin Langworthy's murderer. At the meeting on Friday, May 1, the lawyer E. B. Trumbull introduced a resolution "to the effect $500 be appropriated by the town and placed in the hands of some responsible party to be employed in working up the case."

Since so many residents assumed this plan surely would be adopted, attendance at the meeting was slim. To everyone's surprise, a faction from "the northern part of the town" showed up and presented "strong opposition." The group was headed

---

74 *Stonington Mirror*, April 30, 1874.

by Manasseh Miner from Mystic, Thomas W. Palmer from the Road District, and Thomas Greenman, a partner in his family's shipbuilding enterprise, George Greenman & Co., of Mystic.[75] The *Mirror* reported that the three men spoke against the reward, objecting "to taxing the town, representing that they did so on principle, meaning probably the principal which pays seven per cent." Trumbull's motion was defeated 19 to 22.

The *Mirror*'s Jerome Anderson could hardly contain his outrage, even six days later. "We speak only the opinion of all liberal right minded men when we say that the town was disgraced by this action. . . .Shall we allow the miserable penuriousness of a few men to prevent [justice] being done? It is a stain upon the records of this town." He maintained that a complete and thorough investigation was needed to come up with stronger evidence against Libby or to uncover a more likely new murder suspect. "The question is can murder be committed here with impunity," Anderson declaimed.

In 1874, the leading citizens of Stonington were indeed shocked that a murder had taken place in their town. Although statistics are difficult to pinpoint, it appears that no murders had occurred in Stonington or the small surrounding communities since well before the Civil War. A man had been convicted of murder in Norwich in 1871, but Norwich was considered a city.[76] How-

---

75 Manasseh Miner was superintendent of the Quiambog District's Noyes Neck Fish Works and lived on Church Street in Mystic. Thomas W. Palmer (1816-1894), a farmer, lived at various times on Flanders Road and Pequot Trail. Thomas S. Greenman (1810-1887) was the youngest of the Greenman brothers in shipbuilding in Mystic. He was known for his "independence of thought and action." (quoted in William N. Peterson, *"Mystic Built,"* p. 38). Both T.W. Palmer and Greenman were active in the Prohibition cause.

76 Wethersfield Prison Records, Connecticut State Library. Between 1845 and 1875, no one from Stonington was convicted of murder. In 1871, Alexander Montgomery of Norwich was convicted of murder. In the early 1850s, one New London man and one Norwich man were convicted of murder in the second degree.

ever, Jerome Anderson was confident that the citizens of Stonington were safe. "No one believes that there is greater danger of murder in the town today than there was a month ago." It was "the honor and reputation of our town abroad" that needed protection.

The men who opposed the reward accepted the probability that the murderer was already under lock and key in New London. Why bother to spend more time and taxpayer money looking further? As the *New London Evening Telegram* reported, Tom Palmer contended that since "we had Libby sure, the proper thing to do would be to knock him in the head and waste no money in the matter." Thomas Greenman "objected to establishing a precedent." Characterized by the paper as an absent-minded professor, Manasseh Miner "wandered around the universe in an unsteady manner demonstrating finally that a mill tax was in direct antagonism with the cosmic forces and the true solution of the molecular and atomic theories."[77]

Reluctant to admit defeat, the Stonington selectmen called for another town meeting on the following Tuesday, May 5. This time, they were going to be sure to circulate the petition throughout the town, including the Mystic area. Nevertheless, the New London paper took pleasure in mocking Stonington's predicament: "The American eagle is roused in this bailiwick and exhibits a tendency to claw things. As the old Romans used to put it so quaintly, there'll be h—ll to pay next week."[78]

"STONINGTON IN A WORSE WAY" was the *Mirror*'s headline on May 14. Jerome Anderson seemed to turn Stonington into the victim, forgetting about the unfortunate Irvin Langworthy. "The gentlemen who believe that $500 is worth more than

---

77 *New London Evening Telegram*, May 5, 1874.
78 Ibid.

the good name of the town beat up recruits enough to defeat the resolution appropriating that amount to be used in working up the Langworthy murder." Anderson was speechless with indignation, petulantly stating, "We don't care to publish the disgrace of the town." The reward had been opposed "wholly on sectional grounds—Mystic against Stonington."

As the meeting came to an abrupt close, Thomas W. Palmer offered, as a consolation, a set of resolutions censuring the out-of-town newspapers, and specifically the *New York Times*, for their cruel and "deeply wounding…insidious attacks" against his friend Henry Langworthy. Ridiculing Palmer's spelling and grammar, Anderson characterized the resolutions as "asinine," although he published them "verbatim, et literatim, et spellatim, et punctuatim." However, Palmer's points were basically the same ones Anderson had made himself two weeks earlier. In his resolutions, Palmer complained that the *Times*'s "missrepresentations and Mean insinuations" were "dastardly and Malicious copable [sic] of downright injury and injustice." The *Mirror*'s editor was chiefly worried that "our best and wealthiest citizens here have been insulted by a crowd of irresponsibles…and the town made the laughing stock of the state."[79]

In fact, the reputation of Stonington was under attack, but it was no laughing matter. The superior court in New London had appointed lawyers to represent the incarcerated William Libby.[80] His attorneys Ralph Wheeler and Charles W. Butler called the inquest a "farce before the Stonington justice of the peace which

---

79   *Stonington Mirror*, May 14, 1874.

80   Although Libby did have the benefit of a court appointed lawyer, it was only in 1917 that Connecticut became the first state in the union to adopt the public defender system on a statewide basis.

has been dignified by the name of an examination."[81] They complained that Libby had never been read his rights, had never been given the opportunity to request counsel, and had never been properly put to plea. It is not clear whether the New London lawyer Oscar Hewitt intended to act as counsel when he visited Libby in his cell the day after the murder or whether he was there to facilitate Tibbits's reporting. But Wheeler and Butler, now on the case, were indignant that Libby had been accused and bound over before the inquest jury even finished hearing testimony.

The verdict, establishing murder as the cause of death, did not even imply that he was a suspect. "Where the justice gets his authority for such a novel and expeditious method of transacting criminal business is a question which cannot be very satisfactorily answered," the attorneys complained. A proper hearing and examination of the facts, such as would occur before a grand jury, had not been conducted, and the man had been "thrown in jail without the observance of the necessary legal formalities and upon mere hearsay and reputation." The attorneys called for an explanation from Justice Palmer and stated that "public opinion as to the administration of justice in Stonington will scarcely be of a favorable nature."[82]

However, the prisoner was encountering a problem of gaining access to his attorneys in New London as well. During the first week in May, when Sheriff Raymond visited Libby in jail, Libby told him "a story which differed materially from his testimony

---

81   Ralph Wheeler was a lawyer in New London with offices at 55 State Street. In the fall of 1874, he was elected a Connecticut state senator. Charles W. Butler was a partner in Belcher & Butler at 60 1/2 State Street, New London. This firm represented the defense in many New London police court cases.

82   *New London Evening Telegram*, April 28, 1874.

before the jury of inquest." Thereupon, Raymond ordered the jailer to bar all visitors, including the attorneys, Wheeler and Butler. The sheriff was of the opinion that admission to the jail by counsel was "a matter of privilege." The two attorneys had to exert pressure on Raymond to issue them a written pass.[83] Proclaiming that this "loose and careless way of transacting criminal business is a disgrace to the civilization of the 19th century," they stated that even "the poorest and humblest citizen" had the right to protection under the law. The opinion around New London seemed to be that Libby could have secured a writ of habeas corpus had he had a few friends or the sum of $100.[84]

William B. Libby certainly did not possess $100, nor did he have the benefit of backing from friends or family. As he had claimed, his father actually did live a few miles east of Lewiston, Maine. Simeon Turner Libby owned a farm on No Name Pond Road near Sabattus, also known at the time as the town of Webster. William was the third child of Simeon and Harriet McKenney Libby, but his mother had died giving birth to her eighth child in 1865. Libby had told the Stonington inquest jury that he had a stepmother, but, in fact, his father did not officially remarry until June 1874, two months after William's arrest.[85]

The *Lewiston Evening Journal* carried the murder story on Tuesday, April 21, 1874, and reported two days later that "Libby,

---

83   Ibid., May 8, 1874.
84   Ibid., April 28, 1874.
85   Charles T. Libby, *Libby Family in America, 1602-1881* (Portland, Maine, 1882), p. 516. Sanford Everts & Co., *Atlas and History of Androscoggin County, Maine,* (Philadelphia, 1873), pp. 30, 31, 85. *Lewiston–Auburn Directory, 1874-1875* (Boston: Greenough Jones & Co., 1874). There are a great many Libby families in Maine, and there were fifteen Libbys listed in the 1874 Lewiston–Auburn Directory, including pastors, a councilman, and teachers. S.T. Libby apparently did some masonry work as well as farming. He married Mary A. Carney in June 1874.

the supposed murderer of Irving Langworthy at Stonington, Connecticut, claims a residence in Lewiston."[86] However, it is unknown whether Simeon Libby ever noticed this revelation in the "City and Country" column, or, if he did, whether he communicated with his son. What does appear to be the case is that there was no one to support William Libby as he waited in jail.

MOREOVER, "A LANGWORTHY RELATIVE," Peleg Clarke Jr., a resident of Westerly and the husband of Maria Langworthy's twin sister Mary, came forward to outline in detail what he understood to be the truth about Libby. At the same time, he obviously hoped to dispel some of the rumors clouding the reputation of Henry Langworthy. According to a letter from Clarke that was published in Westerly's *Narragansett Weekly*, Libby had indeed met Henry Langworthy outside Henry Stanton's store in October. The stranger had offered to work for room and board through the winter, but Henry Langworthy had insisted that when the weather allowed for farm work, he would pay Libby $10 a month. When the weather closed in during mid-winter, Libby could do chores around the place to earn his keep. Clarke stated that Libby had always frightened Maria Langworthy and "some of her friends" as well. These friends—perhaps his own wife—"would not be comfortable staying overnight" if Libby remained in the house.[87]

---

86   *Lewiston Evening Journal*, April 21, 24, 1874.

87   *Narragansett Weekly*, April 30, 1874. The *Narragansett Weekly* was the precursor of the *Westerly Sun*. Peleg Clarke, Jr., was born in Hopkinton, Rhode Island, in 1819, and his family moved shortly thereafter to Stonington. In 1835, he became a carpenter's apprentice in Westerly, and by 1843 he owned his own lumber business, planing mill, and sash and blind factory on Main Street in Westerly. He became an architect and engineer, responsible for many buildings and residences in the Westerly area, including the White Rock Mill and village (1849) and the Dixon House (1867), a five-story hotel that stood next to the Washington Trust Company. The Dixon House burned down in 1928. He married Mary Taylor Clarke in 1839, the same year that her sister, Maria, married Henry D. Langworthy. The *Westerly Sun*, October 16, 1899.

Peleg Clarke had more to say about Libby's character. He had seen the hired man "use stock roughly," and Henry Langworthy had reprimanded him for it. At one point, Libby had broken a six-tined pitchfork over the head of a cow. When Henry Langworthy discovered the broken implement, Libby had tried to pin the deed on "Mr. Loper's man who was driving a cow on Mr. Langworthy's property." The Loper employee was interrogated, and he reported that Libby had done it and, furthermore, that Courtland had witnessed the act. Courtland then confirmed the story, whereupon Libby, furious with Courtland, continued to deny it. According to Clarke, there were other "matters of even less importance" which had also contributed to "misunderstandings" between Courtland and Libby.

As for Irvin's relationship with the hired man, Clarke remarked on more "numerous crossings." Since Irvin attended the Mystic Valley Institute during the winter term, he had spent less time around Libby. However, Irvin would "frequently ask [Libby] to do chores for him, such as to hitch his horse to the buggy, put up feed for him to carry for his horse . . .and to do such favors as would gain time in getting to school, but Libby almost as frequently refused."

Since the murder, rumors had been circulating concerning Irvin, Libby, and the killing of a dog. Clarke wished to set that record straight. Apparently, Samuel C. Langworthy had a very old dog, and he asked Libby to shoot it. He also had agreed to pay Libby's price of twenty-five cents. When Libby asked Irvin for his father's shotgun, Irvin inquired why he needed it. Upon discovering that Libby was going to shoot his cousin's dog, Irvin "told him he could not do it on his father's premises" and "would not let go the gun." Libby made threatening remarks to Irvin, but the boy sloughed them off. The Saturday before the murder, Irvin discounted concerns about Libby's animosity, but "others" feared that "something awful would take place."

• **Mystery and Rumors**

In Peleg Clarke's mind, Libby was, without "the slightest doubt," guilty of the murder of Irvin and the assault against Courtland. Clarke believed that Libby had planned all along to murder Mr. and Mrs. Langworthy. This would explain why Henry Langworthy's shotgun was found in the carriage house. Libby must have been planning to shoot Langworthy when he put up his horse that Sunday night. The whiffletree could have been placed behind the stove for only one purpose, "to dispatch Mrs. Langworthy." The matches had all been removed from the kitchen "to prevent her striking a light to see her murdered son" before the perpetrator bludgeoned her. It all seemed a logical scenario to Clarke.

However, Libby had made no attempt to kill Mr. or Mrs. Langworthy. What is puzzling about Libby is that he did not try to escape from the Darling Hill farm before the Langworthys returned home. But where was he going to go? He knew almost no one in the area other than Langworthy friends and relatives. More to the point, he probably trusted no one. It was too late to board a packet boat or a train, even if he had the money for a ticket. Considering his situation, would he have had a general knowledge of the roads in this unfamiliar section of New England? Rather than run, he chose to stay at Darling Hill and portray himself as being victimized along with Irvin and Courtland. Libby seemed to have total confidence that the Langworthys would believe his story, would see him as a member of the Darling Hill family attacked by outsiders.

When Jerome Anderson was searching for a motive in the murder, he stated that it seemed unlikely Libby would attack two men with whom he had been "on almost fraternal terms."[88] Fraternal? The relationships that Peleg Clarke described did not

---

88   *Stonington Mirror*, April 23, 1874.

sound brotherly. Hamilton Langworthy had told the inquest jury that his brothers and Libby had disputes such as were likely to occur "in any family." Did Hamilton consider Libby to be a family member? Apparently, Libby "was warmly attached" to Hamilton, considering him "the only decent man in the family."[89] But Irvin, and even Courtland, evidently treated Libby as just a hired hand, not as a family member or a brother. A reporter in the *Hartford Times*, attempting to account for the ill feeling between Irvin and Libby, put it as "the former being rather domineering and latter inclined to be obstinate and resentful."[90]

IN AN ERA NOT YET familiar with modern psychology, this explanation was remarkably insightful and unclouded by the preoccupation with mystery. William Libby had two older brothers and three younger ones.[91] His relationships with his father and brothers probably will never be known, but they doubtless must have figured significantly in his upbringing. Today, an investigation might also focus on the class differences between Libby and the Langworthy sons. How intensely did Libby resent being treated as a servant? How much did he long to be included in the family as an equal? It appears that the Stonington inquest jury overlooked all of these issues as they considered the Langworthy tragedy.

While William Libby had been truthful about most of his background, he withheld certain key facts. He stated at the inquest that he had been in the Navy for the normal term of three years,

---

89 *Hartford Times*, April 25, 1874.

90 Ibid.

91 William Libby had two older brothers, Alexander and Charles, and three younger, Frank, Jacob, and Joel. He also had a younger sister, Rosanna. Another sister, Pedora, died the day she was born, June 8, 1862. His mother, Harriet, died in 1865 giving birth to Joel. *Libby Family in America*, p. 516.

implying that he enlisted in 1870. However, records show that he actually enlisted on August 30, 1872, for three years. Therefore, by the fall of 1873, when he appeared in Stonington, he would have only served slightly more than one year. He was first listed on the vessel *Worcester* but boarded the *Canandaigua* on December 7, 1872, as a "Landsman."[92] What exactly had occurred during the following year? Why had he suddenly left the Navy and chosen to keep it a secret? The circumstances of his early departure from the Navy were never officially recorded.

More significant was the matter of Libby's age. He told the inquest jury that he was twenty-two. Others guessed him to be somewhere between twenty-four and thirty. Reporters continually referred to him as "the man Libby." However, he was actually born on October 9, 1853, which made him only twenty in the spring of 1874, a mere three years older than Irvin Langworthy.[93] He was then only eighteen at the time he enlisted in the Navy, but his naval records list him as twenty-one. Libby evidently wanted people to think that he was older, but once he got into trouble in Stonington, that might not have been a smart tactic. The possibility exists that he might have been subject to quite different treatment had the authorities known that he was twenty, still considered a minor or "infant" under Connecticut law. The severity of the crime affected treatment of juvenile criminals, and Connecticut courts began assigning guardians to juvenile prisoners in the 1830s.[94] In any event, no one seemed to be concerned enough to check on Libby's age or appoint a guardian for him. He was simply assumed to be adult and responsible for his actions.

---

92 Record Group 24, Records of the Bureau of Naval Personnel (Muster Rolls and Enlistment Returns), National Archives.

93 *Libby Family in America*, p. 516.

94 Nancy Hathaway Steenburg, *Children and the Criminal Law in Connecticut, 1635-1855, Changing Perceptions of Childhood.* (New York: Routledge, 2005).

Mystery and Rumors • 53

It was not until the September term of the Superior Court that a grand jury could be summoned to examine the evidence surrounding Irvin Langworthy's murder. The state's attorney for New London County, Daniel Chadwick,[95] had framed an indictment against William Libby. Chadwick, an 1845 graduate of Yale, had studied law with his uncle, Connecticut Chief Justice Henry M. Waite, as well as Lafayette Foster, a renowned lawyer in Norwich. He had been a member of both the Connecticut State Senate and House and was practicing law in Lyme.[96]

On September 14, 1874, a jury of fourteen men from the county—not one from Stonington, however—was sworn in before Superior Court Judge Edward I. Sanford of New Haven at the courthouse in New London. Once the judge completed his meticulous charge, the grand jury got down to questioning important witnesses in the case, including Henry and Maria Langworthy, Courtland, the doctors, and several neighbors.

The *New London Evening Telegram*'s reporter, perhaps Tibbits himself, remarked that, after nearly five months in jail, "the prisoner Libby has altered very much in appearance since his confinement. He has lost considerable flesh and his once ruddy complexion has given place to an almost ghastly hue."[97] At about

---

95   Daniel Chadwick was born in Lyme, Connecticut, in 1825. He was state's attorney for New London County for fourteen years. In 1880, he became U. S. attorney for Connecticut.

96   Henry Matson Waite (1787-1869) practiced in Lyme and was chief justice of the state from 1854 to 1857. His son, Morrison R. Waite, was unanimously elected Chief Justice of the United States in January 1874 and served until 1888. Lafayette Foster (1806-1880), a Norwich lawyer, was at various times speaker of the State House of Representatives, mayor of Norwich, and a Republican U.S. senator. As president pro tempore of U. S. Senate in April 1865, he became the acting vice president of the United States when Andrew Johnson succeeded to the presidency after Lincoln's assassination.

97   *New London Evening Telegram*, September 14, 1874.

4 p.m., the grand jury concluded its deliberations, finding the indictment against Libby to be "a true bill." The following week, the defense counsel moved to have the case continued until the Superior Court's November term, which was scheduled to take place in Norwich. Thus, the young Maine native, William Libby, spent his twenty-first birthday, October 9, in the jail in New London, Connecticut.

ON DARLING HILL, Henry Langworthy carried on with the business of farming. He rehired a former hand named Hazard to replace Libby, and his son Hamilton also pitched in to help. However, the year continued to be fraught with calamity. On Tuesday, October 27, "as Hamilton and Hazard were driving westward towards Mystic, a team drove up at a furious speed behind and in attempting to pass, struck their wagon, smashing the wheels, upsetting the two men in the ditch and disengaging the horse who started off on a run." Hamilton was able to catch up with the horse in Nathan Noyes's yard, but when he got back to the wagon, he "found Mr. Hazard still on the ground with his leg broken." The speeding team had made no attempt to stop, and the *Mystic Press* labeled this sort of recklessness "criminal."[98]

---

98 *Mystic Press,* October 30, 1874.

2. The Trial

New London County Courthouse, 1934 Historic American Buildings Survey photo

In the mid-1870s, a murder case tried at the New London County Courthouse attracted intense press attention, just as murder cases do today. Courtrooms were filled to capacity. For those who did not attend, the evening newspapers provided the sole source of information recreating each day's proceedings, a function now shared with local television and cable news. The Libby trial had been anticipated with great interest throughout the county, and the press saw an opportunity to satisfy a waiting audience. Crowded court docket schedules prevented the trial from taking place during the November term in Norwich; thus, *State v. William Libby* became the first case on the criminal docket of the Superior Court for the January 1875 term in New London. Predictably, the city's *Evening Telegram* touted the "GREAT MURDER CASE," as editor John Tibbits boldly stated: "The trial promises to be one of the most exciting ever known in this state."[99]

The *New London Evening Telegram* sent a stenographer into the courtroom to cover every session, with the result that today we have a word-for-word record of the witnesses' responses as well

---

99   *New London Evening Telegram,* January 18, 1875.

as the attorneys' closing arguments and the judge's charge to the jury. Unfortunately, the reporter omitted the questions that attorneys asked the witnesses. Still, the newspaper's multi-column daily record provides us with two vivid pictures, one being what occurred at the Darling Hill farm leading up to and on the night of April 19, 1874. At the same time, the transcript informs our understanding of nineteenth-century rural life. We are presented with details of day-to-day farm routines and, more specifically, a bird's-eye view of the Quiambog hamlet. Additionally, the testimony affords us a unique opportunity to hear the voices of everyone involved in the tragic event.

THE LIBBY TRIAL COMMENCED at 2 p.m. on Tuesday, January 19, 1875, at the New London County Courthouse. This handsome gambrel-roofed building, where reputedly Patrick Henry argued cases, Daniel Webster spoke, and Horace Greeley campaigned for Abraham Lincoln, was constructed in 1784. The courthouse stood, as it still does today, at the top of the hill facing State Street in New London. In 1875, before a wing was added onto the rear of the building, the Superior Court convened in a large room, with a gallery around three sides, on the second floor.[100]

Part of the delay in scheduling the trial may have had to do with the fact that a judge of the State Supreme Court was required to sit as an associate judge on murder trials.[101] Therefore, the chief justice of the Connecticut Supreme Court, John Duane Park, presided over Libby's trial beside Superior Court Judge Earl Martin of Killingly. The fifty-five-year-old Park had studied law with the elder statesman Lafayette Foster in the mid-1840s

---

100 The interior of the courthouse, especially the second floor, has been remodeled several times.
101 *Stonington Mirror*, January 14, 1875.

and represented Norwich in the state legislature prior to being elected Connecticut chief justice in 1872.[102]

STATE'S ATTORNEY DANIEL CHADWICK had expected to be assisted in the prosecution by Jeremiah Halsey of Norwich. However, Halsey was ill, and the venerable John T. Wait replaced him as assistant prosecuting attorney. Wait, another student of Lafayette Foster, had himself been state's attorney for New London County, a state senator, and, since 1867, a member of the Connecticut House of Representatives.[103]

As for the defense attorneys, Ralph Wheeler, originally appointed by the court to defend Libby, had been elected to the Connecticut State Senate the previous November. His place as senior defense attorney was turned over to Andrew C. Lippitt, Sr., who practiced law at 19 State Street in New London with his son, Andrew Jr. Charles W. Butler completed the defense team. Perhaps to pique curiosity about the trial, the *Evening Telegram* suggested that "the line of defense will be of a somewhat peculiar and startling nature."[104]

AS USUAL, THE FIRST ORDER of business was jury selection. Although some jurors failed to appear because they had "not been legally summoned" and others had reasons they could not serve,

---

102 *Biographical Review*, vol. 26, p. 345.

103 John Turner Wait (1811-1899) was born in New London but soon moved to Norwich. He studied at Trinity College and was admitted to the bar in 1836. He married Elizabeth Harris in 1842 and was state's attorney for New London County (1842-1844 and 1846-1854). His son, Marvin, was killed at the Battle of Antietam in 1862. In 1876, he was elected as a Republican to the U.S. House of Representatives and served until 1887. *Biographical Review*, vol. 16, p. 128; Hurd, *History of New London County*, p. 49.

104 *New London Evening Telegram*, January 18, 1875.

• The Trial

a jury was impaneled on Tuesday afternoon. No Stonington men were included, but three Groton residents were chosen, including Nathan Sands Fish. Fish, who had a large farm on Poquonnock plain, was the nephew of a Mystic shipbuilder and bank president, Nathan G. Fish, and had himself been a store owner in Mystic. The family also had ties to the Union Baptist Church and, no doubt, had a passing acquaintance with Henry Langworthy. Nevertheless, Nathan S. Fish was selected, with his fellow Groton residents James D. Avery and James Turner. Other jurors included John Richards, Abraham Bragaw, and Franklin P. Kenyon of New London; W. L. Peckham, Oliver Maxson, S. G. Jerome, and John Bradbury of Waterford; Curtis M. Smith of East Lyme; and Henry W. Brainerd of Old Lyme. When questioned, none of the jury members expressed any "conscientious scruples against hanging."[105]

As THE LIBBY TRIAL got under way in earnest on Wednesday morning, the courtroom was "crowded to excess."[106] The majority of the crowd traveled by local train service from Stonington and Mystic to New London very early in the morning. Of course, in 1875 this entailed a ferry ride across the Thames and for most a long uphill walk from the ferry dock to the courthouse, followed by the reverse trek in the late afternoon. Luckily, the January weather was not particularly harsh that year.[107]

Once Judge Martin called the court to order, the charges against

---

105 Ibid., January 20, 1875.
106 *Mystic Press*, January 22, 1875.
107 *Stonington Mirror*, January 28, 1875. The paper reported that the first week of the trial "one train carried ninety Stonington and Mystic residents to New London." The *New London Evening Telegram* listed train schedules: Stonington to New London at 5:45 a.m., return to Stonington 7:20 p.m. The first railroad bridge over the Thames was not built until 1889.

Libby were read out. The accused, whose appearance had "materially altered since his imprisonment," pleaded not guilty. Daniel Chadwick then made a brief opening statement and called Henry Clay Palmer, an architect with an office at 106 Water Street in Stonington Borough, to the stand. The prosecution had asked Palmer to draw up plans of the Langworthy house and farm buildings, and a diagram of the Darling Hill area. The young man produced the drawings and explained them to the judges, jury, and counselors, giving special emphasis to the first and second floors of the kitchen ell. The plans, which now appear to be lost, remained in full view in order to illustrate the testimony of subsequent witnesses.

The sixty-five-year-old Henry D. Langworthy was the first material witness sworn in. Attorney Chadwick asked the father of the murdered boy to relate what happened on Sunday night, April 19. Langworthy had testified before the inquest jury as well as the grand jury and now retold his story in a laconic and unemotional manner. As he and his wife were returning from church in Mystic sometime after 10 p.m., he said,

> we reached about this point [referring to a diagram of the road] when my wife says someone called your name. The horse was not at a run, but a quick trot. After we reached the gate, I touched up my horse and went on at a quick run. As we reached the steps my wife jumped out. I went to the barn with my horse. As I turned about, Libby met me. He says, "Mr. Langworthy, there are robbers in the house; they have battered Irvin. I have fought them as long as I could and I am going to lie down here and die." He did lie down on the floor. This was all done as quick as words could speak it; knowing that if the robbers were in the house my wife was in danger, I hastened there.[108]

---

108 *New London Evening Telegram*, January 20, 1875.

As Langworthy went on, he conveyed the bewilderment and sudden trepidation that the couple felt as they tried to understand what had gone on in their absence:

> I went through the first and second doors [again referring to Palmer's diagram] and saw my wife standing by the closet. She asked me if I had any matches in my pocket. I said no and [told her] that Libby had said there were robbers in the house and that they had battered Irvin. There was no light there at this time. My wife said, "There is some one here and I can't wake him up." I asked where. She said, "on the east end of the table." I then went around the table and as I did so Irvin's head struck me about here (near the chest). I put my hands down on his face and said, "Oh they have killed Irvin, he is dead and cold." My wife asked me again if I had any matches; I said no but I could get some. She said, "They are all gone off the shelf and from the closet where we keep them." Then I went to where I generally keep a gross of matches which is right on the shelf over the door of the closet where Mrs. Langworthy stood, found plenty of matches there. I lighted a match and saw the situation of the room, found it as I have said, then looked at the dining room door and saw that it was just ajar. I shut and locked it. By that time my match had gone out. My wife touched me on the sleeve and said, "Come let's go—let's go somewhere—let's go down to Samuel's." We went out, closed the door behind us. My wife says, "Come William, go down with us." I said, "He says he is almost dead." We went down these steps and came along to this gate which leads out of the back yard.[109]

Leaving Libby in the barn, the Langworthys rushed down to

---

109 Ibid.

their nephew Samuel's house, where Henry deposited his wife. At this point, the family feared that the murderer or robbers could be hiding somewhere in the house. After talking Samuel's three hired men into accompanying him, Henry returned to Farmer's Palace. On the witness stand, he pointed to a spot in the barn where he had found his shotgun standing in the corner. He also pointed to where his own hired man still lay in the barn and stated, "I had no conversation with Libby and have not spoken with him from that time to this." Only one of the three young men, William Perkins, dared to enter the house, but he refused to budge from the kitchen entrance and would not venture upstairs with Henry to look for Courtland. Henry testified that he "took a lantern and went up into Courtland's room."

> I found him wallowing in blood, rolling to and fro, the bed was covered with blood. I asked Courtland how he felt. He replied, "I feel sick." Asked him if anyone had struck him and he said no. I examined the wound on the back of his head, saw that he had bled all he could bleed in one sense. I then went downstairs and went out, not being able to get the boys to stay. I went back to Samuel's after closing the doors behind me.[110]

Finally, Henry was able to persuade his nephew to go back up to house with him and search for the supposed robbers. Samuel examined Irvin's body and confirmed that he was "dead and cold." The two then began a systematic tour of the house. Henry said, "We had a lantern with us. I took the lantern and asked Samuel to go ahead with me, saying, 'If they shoot me you'll have the next chance.' Each of us had double-barreled guns, one

---

110 Ibid. Later testimony by Samuel Langworthy indicated that Henry may have been confused here. On a return trip to the house in the company of Samuel, Henry went upstairs. The nephew said they found Courtland wounded in bed, and Henry tried to question his son.

was mine (I had taken it), the other was Samuel's." Later in the trial, during cross-examination, Henry Langworthy explained, "We carried guns for our protection. We did not know what we should meet with. We took them to protect us from robbers." However, they did not encounter any robbers and, furthermore, found that nothing in the rest of the house had been disturbed.

ON THURSDAY, JANUARY 21, when he was called to testify, Henry's nephew, Samuel Langworthy, described in detail what he saw the night of the murder when he accompanied his uncle back to the house:

> We went directly, entering the house by the north door. We had a lantern. The door was closed, both outer and inner doors were closed. Inside, I was first attracted by the corpse of Irvin. I took hold of his hand to feel the pulse and found it cold, then tried the heart—no pulsation and but very little warmth in the bowels... Where Irvin sat, the chair, beneath which there was a large quantity of blood. I should think the wound had bled nearly all it could—occasionally there was a drop. The head was thrown back as far as its weight could carry it. He was in a reclining position, his feet on the lounge [sofa]. He was maybe eighteen inches from the lamp. Neither carpet nor anything else was apparently out of order; no indications of a struggle. Irvin had nothing in his hand but between his limbs, which were extended about a foot apart, there was a book. Saw no paper on the table or floor. Recollect one chair sitting up by the sink. After examining the kitchen, we went into the front part of the house. The rooms upstairs were apparently all right. The doors were generally closed. We went next up the back stairs... Found Courtland upstairs seemingly insensible. His father asked him if he was badly hurt. He did not seem to realize

that a question had been asked him. There were marks of wounds about him. There was nothing to indicate that anything had been taken from the house. I sent a man for aid, sent for a doctor, asking him to come immediately.[111]

AFTER ADJOURNING for lunch on Wednesday, the trial resumed. Upon being sworn in again, Henry Langworthy was asked to describe the scene in the kitchen when he and his wife returned that night and the exact position of his murdered son. Irvin had been "sitting at the east end of the table, his right elbow resting thereon." Henry then produced a tape measure marking the exact dimensions of the table, sixty inches long and forty-two inches wide, and identified the exact position of the lamp by referring to a table in the courtroom. He maintained that the whiffletree, which was found "standing by the mantel," had been in the wood shed when he left the farm that night. Regarding the drill, Henry said, "We had two kinds of iron drills about the place, one we used on rocks and another was known as a churn drill." The drills were then presented as evidence. Henry was certain that the drill in question (it is not clear which of the two) had been in the wood shed also, and he did not remember seeing it on the night of the murder.

Under cross-examination, Henry Langworthy described the kitchen in greater detail:

> The table had leaves… I found it open when I came in that night. Distance between the table and the stove was about four feet. This stove is for cooking purposes. The lid part of the stove is on the south side towards the table. Two windows are on the east side, four or five feet apart. Between the windows, there was a looking glass and a rack

---

111 Ibid., January 22, 1875.

for papers. There were green wooden blinds on that side of the house. I noticed that the blinds were open on both these windows. Blinds on the other side were open also. The lamp had no shade, just a chimney. Noticed it was broken on the side to the east. It was standing about opposite where my son sat; it was broken upon the side where my son sat, I suppose by a blow from that side.[112]

When asked about the family dogs, Henry Langworthy said that the two dogs had been locked in the back part of the ell. "The dogs had been trained to bark whenever any one approached the door. They were kept mostly as watchdogs. These dogs universally bark upon persons approaching the door of an evening. I have no remembrance of their ever failing to do so."[113]

DEFENSE ATTORNEY Andrew Lippitt saw quite clearly that his function was to interrupt the prosecution's narrative and to create doubts about Libby's role in the murder. Thus, he quickly changed the subject as he cross-examined Henry Langworthy, questioning him about his practice of hiring occasional laborers. Lippitt asked Henry to list all the men he had employed in the previous three years. Henry replied, "I am 65 [and have] been in good health [but] my memory is not strong. I need to refer to my books." Unwittingly playing into Lippitt's hands, he went on, "I can't say from what places my workmen have come." He admitted to hiring at least five or six men, perhaps more, for short periods, among them two tramps. Referring to some notes, he began to list some of his employees. A Perkins had to be fired after a month as he was "said to be dishonest." One named Hazard had come from Newport. Mosier from Stonington had been

---

112 Ibid. 20 Jan. 1875.
113 Ibid.

discharged after two months but then rehired.[114] Frank Williams, on the other hand, had worked for the Langworthys for two years, and Hamilton Langworthy had seen him since and even lent him money. Henry Langworthy could not remember who exactly had been at the farm the previous summer or winter.

Regarding Libby, however, he testified that he had not hired him on the spot but "said [he] might." He also made no bargain with Libby regarding work, despite what his brother-in-law Peleg Clarke had maintained in his letter. He promised to bring in to the court the next day "the best list of men working for me that I can for three years prior to the murder."[115]

When Henry Langworthy was recalled on Thursday to complete his testimony about hired farm hands, he did produce a written list. Walter Langdon of Stonington had lived at the farm for one three-month season and was then dismissed for unsatisfactory work. Another Stonington man, John Brown, had been a day worker. Two years back, Ezekiel Corey of Kingston, Rhode Island, was hired and worked for a month before being fired. The seventeen-year-old Dewey boy and "his crony" Mosier had lived one season at the farm, but Maria Langworthy had fired them for being insolent one day when Henry was away.[116] Upon returning, Henry also had fired Frank Perkins for remarking to Dewey and Mosier that they should tell Maria "to shut up her

---

114 Although the newspaper spelled this name Mosier, it might well have been Mosher. There was a Mosher family in Stonington at the time. *Anderson's 1881 Stonington Directory* lists Charles and Henry Mosher boarding at 21 Water Street and John Mosher boarding at 7 Water Street.

115 *New London Evening Telegram,* January 20, 1875.

116 Haynes, *Stonington Chronology,* has the following entry under March 1870: "Warren Palmer built a house at Wamphassett Pt., Nelson Dewey, tenant; started farm and stock-raising; began charging local farmers for seaweed they had hauled from his shore many years for use as fertilizer." The Dewey boy might have been related to this Nelson Dewey.

head." Only Frank Williams, who now lived in Westerly, had stayed for an extended period, two years, during which he slept in the northwest bedroom of the farmhouse.

Attorney Lippitt did not need to pursue this line of questioning any further. Obviously, a substantial number of men, some with dubious backgrounds, had worked at the Darling Hill Farm. They were all familiar with the house and each family member. Any one of them who had been fired might have had a compelling motive to take revenge on the family.[117] Again, Henry was asked to clarify his terms of employment with Libby. "I said I would give him $20 a month if he would live peaceably and have no grudge against Irvin," he explained, adding that Libby said he had no grudge.[118]

MARIA LANGWORTHY also testified on Thursday, and despite the shocking events of that Sunday night in April she seemed to have a firm grasp on many relevant details. She remembered that when she and her husband left the farm, she "told Irvin, as he let us out of the gate, to clear off the table after Libby and my other son had had tea." Later that night, as the couple made their way up Darling Hill near Samuel Langworthy's house, she heard a call coming from "over the wall" and realized that there was someone running after them. Although Maria did tell her husband to "hurry the horse," she insisted upon correcting the record. "I did not take hold of the reins," she stated, making clear that she considered Henry perfectly capable.

When they came to the house, she "alighted" and knocked on the door. The dogs growled, and as she knocked louder the dogs began to bark "furiously." Perhaps Maria sensed at that moment

---

117 *New London Evening Telegram*, January 21, 1875.
118 Ibid., January 22, 1875.

that something was wrong, because she testified that "customarily" Libby let the dogs outside after 8 p.m. She also explained that the family had two dogs, one about twelve or thirteen years old. The other was "almost a year and not a common cur, but what is called an English setter." Libby had trained this puppy.[119]

Maria testified that she entered the kitchen and immediately smelled kerosene. Going toward a shelf to find the matches, she accidentally bumped into a chair in the dark. The moon, she noted, was almost down and "would not light the room."[120] She then turned toward the closet and "struck a form as I was passing, a form so heavy I supposed it Libby's." She touched the person on the shoulder and, thinking it was Libby asleep, "stepped over [his] limbs as they rested on the sofa." Without realizing it, she had stepped over the legs of her murdered son. Maria recalled that the fire in the stove was almost out, and that she had not noticed any newspapers on the floor, which she described as partly covered with oilcloth and two widths of carpet running east and west.

She then tried to answer a question from Attorney Chadwick regarding why she had not returned to the house later with Henry. She started to say that she had wished to go back, but that Mrs. Samuel Langworthy had thought it "an imprudent act." The defense quickly objected to this testimony, saying that it was irrelevant.[121]

---

119   Ibid., January 21, 1875.

120   By 9 p.m. on April 19, 1874, the three-day-old waxing crescent moon would have contributed little light as at that time it would have stood only 17 degrees above the WNW horizon and only 17 percent of the moon's disk would have appeared illuminated. Mrs. Langworthy was in her kitchen at 10 p.m. so it would have been even darker. D.L. Treworgy, Planetarium Supervisor, Mystic Seaport.

121   *New London Evening Telegram,* January 21, 1875.

Daniel Chadwick subsequently changed his line of questioning, asking Maria Langworthy to describe her son Irvin's relationship with Libby. She replied that the two had been on good terms until the incident involving Libby's shooting Samuel's old dog. After that, she said, Libby "appeared not the same" toward Irvin. She went on, "Libby threatened Irvin with regard to the dog. Irvin told me so." The defense objected to this statement as hearsay.

Irvin Langworthy had evidently taken the spring term off from the Mystic Valley Institute to help around the family farm. However, two days before the murder, Libby told Maria that he thought Irvin was lonely and missed his school. If Libby did resent the way that Irvin treated him, was this suggestion a way of getting Irvin off the farm? Maria stated that she was taken aback and had said to her son, "Oh Irvin, your father is becoming advanced in age and looks to you as his stay and support." Libby might have seen that his tactic did not work. Again, the defense counsel objected to her testimony. However, Maria was able to get the point across that, in several instances over the days leading up to the murder, Libby "looked to me terrible and I was frightened." She was so alarmed that she asked her husband to reload his gun, which "was always kept behind the [linen] press door that opened into the bedroom." In fact, she remembered seeing the gun in that spot on Sunday morning. She "thought Libby a suspicious character [and] began to suspect him at the time he began to grow slack."

Maria ended by giving evidence of her remorse. "When I went away from home on the day of the murder, I left Libby with the son against whom I suppose he had a grudge."[122]

---

[122] Ibid. Regarding the gun, Manasseh Miner was later called as a witness for the defense to testify that Henry Langworthy had been uncertain whether he had returned the gun to the bedroom after using it on Friday. Miner had gone to the farm on Monday morning. However, by Tuesday morning, he said, Henry was "positive that the gun was carried back to the room." *New London Evening Telegram,* January 23, 1875.

ON THE NIGHT of the murder, Samuel Langworthy had sent one of his men down to Stonington Borough to summon the doctor and the constable. Dr. Charles Erskine Brayton, accompanied by his brother Atwood, arrived at Farmer's Palace about a half an hour later, just after midnight.[123] The twenty-three-year-old Dr. Brayton testified, "Mr. Henry Langworthy met me at the door. I entered, laid down my cane and had my attention called to the dead body." Upstairs, Brayton found Courtland "lying still on the bed covered with blood from head to waist."

> There was a clock above the headboard. I cut off some of the man's long hair, cleared the head of clotted blood, bandaged it. [He had] a cut on the back of his head, left side, 2 3/4 inches long, to a depth of 2 1/2 inches. The next morning I noticed contusions about the eye and left ear. [He had] exhibitions of nervousness weeks after.

After being summoned back to the kitchen, Dr. Brayton said, he found William Libby there and examined him.

> He was partially leaning upon the lounge, his feet to the corpse. He came round the end of the table and sat down in a chair. He said nothing while we were moving him, when seated [he] complained of faintness. He had on a round woolen cap. I found a cut on his left temple nearly one inch in length and a quarter of an inch from his hairline slanting toward his nose, depth to skull, very slight, blood in hair,

---

123 In 1875, Dr. Charles Erskine Brayton (born in 1851) and his brother Atwood W. lived at the Brayton family home, 50 Elm Street. Atwood W. became a mason like his father, Atwood Randall Brayton, and the two were responsible for constructing foundations and several local stone buildings, e.g. Calvary Church and the American Velvet Company. In 1880, Dr. Brayton built a new building at 77 Main St.(now an art gallery), where he maintained a residence and office, with a pharmacy on the first floor, a dental parlor and the G.A.R. Post Hall on the second floor. *Biographical Review*, p. 51.

some on face. He was not bleeding when I saw him. He had a contusion on the front of the crown of the head about three inches, not breaking the skin. No treatment [needed] except a plaster on the forehead. He had an abrasion on the right temple. After that someone suggested the body be laid out. Mr. Tillinghast, Mr. [Thomas] Noyes and myself did this work. Saw at this time that the skull was fractured on its back.

The doctor then gave the jury a long, detailed report of his post-mortem examination of Irvin on Tuesday, April 21. From a three-inch scalp wound, the back of the skull had been fractured open "from the junction of its bone with the spinal column extending forward ten inches." Two other fractures extended from the principal one. The wound, which had "penetrated the superior longitudinal sinus," had been made with "a moderately sharp instrument and heavy, not round."[124]

WHEN CONSTABLE Samuel K. Tillinghast was called to testify on Thursday, January 21, he explained that he had reached the Langworthy farm a short time after the Braytons on the night of the murder. It was revealed later in court that Thomas Noyes accompanied him, but Tillinghast made no mention of this fact on the stand. After briefly examining the crime scene in the kitchen, he went up the back stairs to find Dr. Brayton treating Courtland. As he started to go back downstairs, Tillinghast picked up a cap, which was on the floor of the hall, just outside Courtland's room. The constable then asked Henry Langworthy about his hired man and went out to look for him in the horse barn. "At first, I thought [Libby] was intoxicated," he testified. "He was laying down near the barn stairs; seemed to be rather stupid. I

---

[124] *New London Evening Telegram,* January 21, 1875.

roused him and asked what he knew. I accused him of having been drinking and he said he had only drunk some cider."[125]

AT THIS POINT, Tillinghast handcuffed Libby and escorted him into the farmhouse kitchen. Libby sat on the lounge, not far from Irvin's body, which was still seated "at the southeast corner of the table." He told the constable that, earlier in the evening, he had been sitting reading the *Norwich Advertiser* of April 17. When asked which article he had been reading, Libby replied that it was about the loss of a French steamer.[126] Tillinghast then produced the cap. "Libby took the cap and said it was his." Tillinghast was certain that the man "had no cap on in the barn."

Completing his business at Darling Hill, Tillinghast (and Thomas Noyes) proceeded to take Libby to the Borough lock-up, "but stopped at the livery stable to get a lantern." It was at the livery stable that they, including Libby, first heard about two men in the road, one with a light coat. That information had been reported by Thomas Colbert, the railroad engineer, when he stopped in at the livery stable earlier in the evening. Tillinghast testified that he then locked up Libby and "went in search of Colbert."[127]

During cross-examination, Defense Counsel Lippitt questioned Tillinghast intently. Why had the constable not immediately told

---

125 Ibid., January 22, 1875.

126 The *Norwich Advertiser* of April 17, 1874, has not been located, but the *New London Evening Telegram* of April 14, 1874, reported that the French steamer *Ville du Havre* had collided with the *Europe* and had been lost. On April 16, 1874, the *Evening Telegram* reported "Another Steamship Lost." The French steamship *Amerique*, which had left New York on April 4, foundered between Brest and Havre. All passengers were rescued.

127 *New London Evening Telegram*, January 22, 1875. It is unclear whether the livery was Stanton's at 3 Temple Street or the Wadawanuck Livery at 2 High Street, both in the Borough.

the inquest jury about finding the cap? Why had he waited a week to mention this important detail? Tillinghast replied that he "thought it not policy to tell at the inquest all I knew about the affair." He had held back the information, "kept it in my breast." Yes, he had found the folded newspaper with the article about the French steamer at the bottom of the newspaper rack, but one of the other men at the house that night might have picked it up and put it away. He "supposed Libby was drunk" but could not be certain that the man had said he had cider at supper. Finally, in exasperation, the Borough constable blurted out to the court, "My business is that of a stone-cutter although I have not followed it much latterly. My principal business is that of constable, but I don't claim to be a detective."[128]

THE ONE PERSON who might have been able to relate more fully the circumstances leading up to the murder was called next to take the witness stand. Courtland Langworthy, recovered from the blows he had received the previous April, was asked by both the prosecution and the defense attorneys to tell all he could remember about that fateful Sunday night:

> I was in the barn, milking cows. Libby was milking at the north end and I was at the south end. Libby told [me] to get water for wetting the cut feed and I hung the milk in the well…Libby and I ate together, had biscuit, custard pie and tea. I think Irvin ate with father and mother. I saw no cider. [We ate] by the light of the Argand lamp. No one was about the house that evening except Oliver Denison. My brother washed up the dishes and sat down. Irvin cleared off the table then sat down to read. He was at the east side of the table, Libby was at the northeast, with his hat on. I saw no

---

128 Ibid.

paper. Don't know that Libby took a paper. My brother had a book in his hand on the night...I was about three feet from him. I was sitting, while in the room that night, sitting on one side of the table and [Irvin] on the other but not opposite. My folks, after the murder, asked me where Irvin sat. Irvin had not been smoking that evening; he did sometimes. I fastened the doors with bolts soon after supper. Libby had bothered me about a quarrel; I said to him it was a d—d lie and he said he would knock my head from my shoulders. The dog was played with and then I went to bed upstairs, leaving Libby downstairs. He generally let the dogs out about 8 o'clock. Father has lost a cow and I thought Libby had killed it after killing Irvin. No recollection of anyone coming to my room after I went upstairs and before the murder. The last fair look I had of my brother was just before the time I went to bed.[129]

Courtland reiterated that, before leaving the farm for church, his mother had told him to lock the doors, to "fasten up," before he went to bed. In fact, he confessed that he had forgotten to make this point to the grand jury, and his mother had "replied that I ought to." Maria subsequently told the grand jury herself that the doors had been locked.

From the sound of Courtland's testimony, his relationship with Libby appears to have been strained at best. And Libby's comment about knocking off Courtland's head apparently was more than a gratuitous turn of phrase. When the prosecution asked Courtland about any other quarrels or run-ins with Libby, he was able to describe two instances. In December 1873, Courtland said, he was in the wood shed one morning. It was cold outside, and the door was closed. Libby, who had been working

---

[129] Ibid. An Argand lamp, named for Swiss chemist Aime Argand, had a tubular wick, a glass chimney and reflectors to direct the light.

out in one of the fields removing boulders with Irvin, yanked the wood shed door open. He was looking for the drill and swore that he "shouldn't work with Irvin anymore." Only three days before the murder, Libby, hot and thirsty from working in a field, came back to the house for water. The house seems to have been locked, and he called out to Courtland inside for the dipper to get water from the well. Courtland evidently called back from an upstairs window to "help himself" with some sort of cover that was near the house. Libby was furious, so red-faced with anger that he frightened both Courtland and Maria.

Although Courtland had been labeled in the press as *non compos mentis*, he described the Sunday evening at the farm in careful detail, even noting the crucial evidence that Libby had on his hat. He had not noticed the cider or the newspaper, but he was positive that he had locked the doors. Only once did he stray from the subject, as he wistfully mentioned, "I had an oleander by the window. [That night I] stood by it and saw the moon about 2 or 3 hours high." Without hesitation, the defense objected to this digression as irrelevant. During the cross-examination, however, Defense Attorney Andrew Lippitt pursued a line of questioning specifically designed to weaken Courtland's credibility as a witness. The oldest of the Langworthy children had very poor vision. Some said he was almost blind, and he apparently did not read for pleasure. It is not known whether he wore glasses. In any event, Lippitt asked Courtland if he recognized one of the jurors. Although he was acquainted with Nathan Fish, he could not pick him out of the jury panel. He stated, "I can't recognize countenances," but he went on, "I know you, Mr. Lippitt. Your hair is white, your pants and vest are black, the hair of the person next to you on the left [Atty. Butler] is dark; should think a dozen on this bench [there were only six]; think the coat of that man [Mr. Bragaw] is black." When Courtland was allowed to approach the juror, he realized the coat was brown. Lippitt had made his point. Courtland's testimony might not be entirely reliable.[130]

AT THIS POINT, the prosecution called Samuel Langworthy to testify. After identifying himself as Henry Langworthy's nephew and neighbor, Samuel told how he first came in contact with Libby that night.

> My first knowledge of the murder was Libby's rushing to our east piazza and shaking the door with violence loudly enough to rouse me. He said robbers were at the other house. He appeared there about 16 minutes to 10 o'clock. Libby said he had fought as long as he could and that he was knocked all to pieces. He wanted help and said, "Feel my head." I asked how long the robbers had been there; he said about five minutes. I asked him how they got in. He said they walked in and the first he knew they hit him in the head…. He said his own head was covered with bunches and asked me to feel. I did so and found one bunch on the top of his head and a smaller one near the left temple. Did not see cuts or bleeding. I felt Libby's head and after I saw blood on my hands. He did not come into my house. I told him nobody except my wife and mother were at home and that I could not go. I told him to go to Jeffery's for help and he said they would not come. Gave no reason.

As the two men were standing on the porch, they heard a carriage coming, and Samuel "hurried" Libby "to go and stop it." Samuel could not say with any certainty whether or not Libby had his hat on, but he went on to give his testimony about returning to Farmer's Palace with Henry Langworthy. He identified the three men who came to his house that night as William

---

130 *New London Evening Telegram*, January 22, 1875.

Perkins, John Kane, and James Coleman, but said that the only one he personally saw at Henry's house was Coleman. He did not see any newspapers in the kitchen. Samuel seems to have been suspicious of Libby from the beginning as he ended his testimony by stating that he had helped his uncle search the house with his shotgun only to "gratify Mr. Langworthy." He had not expected to find robbers.[131]

ANOTHER RELATIVE, Maria Langworthy's twin sister, Mary Clarke, was then called to testify. Saturday, April 18, the day before the murder, was their birthday, and Maria had invited Mary to the farm on Darling Hill specifically to see her houseplants. Mrs. Clarke had much to say about the atmosphere she found at the farm.

> Nothing was said about the gun. We passed through the room where it was to see the plants; in doing so we passed through Mrs. Langworthy's room. I think the press door was generally left open; this time it was shut... I saw the gun behind the press door where I had not seen it before. I am positive, the press door was closed. When at the table eating, I noticed that Libby was red and looking very angry. I went out to the milk room where my sister was and told her of the man's appearance, adding, 'I wouldn't were I you, keep him any longer.' Mrs. Langworthy replied that they had been intending to get other help, but added, 'but I don't know where he would be [without his employment at the farm].' When Libby had finished his dinner, he went out. I heard nothing said by him. I heard Mr. Langworthy settling with him saying 'so and so much.' Libby was very red but not even looking up. Don't think he thought of

---

131 Ibid.

striking Mr. Langworthy. Mr. Langworthy in arranging for settling, said to Libby, 'I can either get you clothes or give you the money.' Libby did not reply and that is the reason I looked at him. Mr. Langworthy read over the account; it was not disputed; this account was read from a book. I was alarmed by Libby's appearance and would not stay over night.

The newspaper reported that Mrs. Clarke was under cross-examination when she made this statement. If true, she made a poor choice of witness for Libby's defense.[132]

The architect and builder Peleg Clarke, Mary's husband, took the stand to testify about the door knobs at Farmer's Palace. He stated that "both the knobs to the doors of the kitchen are mineral knobs and quite loose, and the knobs inside are also loose. It would be difficult for any one to enter either door without making a noise that would attract attention." However, Libby had stated that the "robbers" had "walked in" noiselessly. Under cross-examination, Peleg Clarke had to admit that he "had never tried the knobs with the purpose of entering without making noise." Hoping to reinforce the noisy door knob point, Attorney Chadwick called Maria Langworthy to the stand. She backed up her brother-in-law, stating that "it would be difficult to enter without making noise." Seeing an opportunity to refute this testimony, Defense Counsel Lippitt asked Maria if she remembered that when the defense team visited Farmer's Palace, they were able to try the knobs without making any sound. Maria retorted, "I remember that you, Mr. Butler, and Mr. Wheeler were at the house. I don't remember that you opened and shut the doors several times and that I remarked that they made very little noise." The impression one gets of Maria Langworthy is

---

132 Ibid.

that she held her ground, a nineteenth-century woman who was not easily intimidated, even by men in positions of power.

DURING THE TRIAL proceedings, witnesses had mentioned several different men being present at Farmer's Palace on the night of the murder. The prosecution, hoping to verify the Langworthys' testimony and looking for discrepancies in Libby's previous statements, proceeded to put these men on the stand. The first of them was William Perkins. He confirmed that he and two others had accompanied Henry Langworthy back to his house from Samuel's. "I myself went out to the horse barn where I saw Libby. Libby said he was going to lie down and die. I left him and went back into the house. The other men would not go in, saying they would faint if they did. I went in with Mr. Langworthy and stood by the stove. The only light we had was that of a lantern we had taken with us. Did not see in the room any disturbances of furniture." Perkins, no doubt prompted by Attorney Chadwick, related an incident that had taken place three weeks before the murder. "When at Mr. Henry Langworthy's I went into the work shop where I found Hamilton at work. Libby soon came in, said, 'I told you I would shoot Samuel's dog.' The dog was in the yard the day before, and he would have killed it but Irvin prevented him. Said he would have revenge upon the boy for taking away the gun and not letting him shoot."

James Coleman admitted that, although he entered the outer kitchen door that night, he "did not go through the next one, just looked in and went right out." Several hours later, he had been inside the kitchen but saw no newspapers, except in the rack. Dr. Brayton, who was sitting in the front of the courtroom at this moment, was asked if he had seen any newspapers; he replied he had not. On the stand, Atwood Brayton swore that he had not seen a newspaper, nor could he remember even hearing about one.[133]

---

133 Ibid.

The Trial • 83

Thomas Noyes, who had accompanied Constable Tillinghast up to Darling Hill from the Borough, swore that he had not seen a newspaper either. Lippitt then began his cross-examination of Noyes, hoping to do away with the incriminating evidence regarding Libby's hat. But Noyes refused to cooperate. He stated, "Saw Libby on the night of the murder…Libby was on his face. Saw no cap. Saw nothing under his head. I have been in conversation with Mr. Butler and Mr. Wheeler [Libby's original defense team] about the affair." An objection was raised, but Noyes was allowed to go on. "Think Mr. Wheeler and Mr. Butler were told by me that Libby lay on his face when in the barn. Don't recollect saying he lay with his face on his cap." Noyes was not going to be coerced into changing his story about the hat. However, Lippitt finally got him to admit that he was "not sure whether Libby did or did not wear a cap into the house."[134] Notably, throughout the testimony, no one seemed to be very concerned about Libby's physical condition as he lay in the barn that night. Perhaps they simply did not care what happened to him, but more likely they did not believe he would die from such minor wounds.

During his testimony, Constable Tillinghast had mentioned that Captain Thomas Miner was among those who had been called to Farmer's Palace on the night of April 19.[135] Miner, stating that he lived "not far from Henry Langworthy," said that James

---

134 Ibid. According to *Anderson's 1881 Stonington Directory*, Thomas Noyes lived at 23 High Street in Stonington Borough.

135 Captain Thomas Miner (or Minor) lived on the opposite side of Quiambog Cove from Henry Langworthy "precisely where his ancestor Thomas erected his mansion in 1653." Address by Rev. William L. Swan, *Dedication of Wequetequock Burial Ground*, August 31, 1899. The house faced south and "the blue waters of Quiambaug Cove." Wheeler, *Homes of Our Ancestors*, p. 62. Captain Miner donated land to the town for the new Quiambog Road, which passed in front of his house just before the new bridge over the cove. *Mystic Pioneer*, June 15, 1867.

Coleman had been sent to his house to summon him on behalf of the Langworthys. He arrived at the farm just after 11 p.m. and stayed there with Henry and Samuel until sometime between 1 and 2 a.m. He testified that he saw Irvin's body but "no appearance of conflict." He did not see a newspaper but did see "broken lamp pieces on the table, a book on the floor." As for the accused man, Miner "went down to the barn, saw Libby there on the floor. Mr. Tillinghast told him to get up and he then said, 'I can't; I am not able.' Tillinghast told him a second time, pretty sharply, and he rose to his feet. When taken into the house and cared for by Dr. Brayton, he said he was faint and wanted to lie down."[136]

During cross-examination of Thomas Miner, Lippitt was determined to settle the problem of the newspaper. Previous testimony was beginning to indicate that Libby had fabricated the newspaper story to make it appear that he was innocently sitting and reading when "robbers" broke into the house. If he had been hit suddenly over the head, he could hardly have put the newspaper back into the bottom of the rack. Lippitt asked Miner what he knew about the newspaper. "Did hear something about a paper being picked up," Miner replied. "Someone said it was of an old date; heard a remark about one or two papers being picked up. I think Mr. Tillinghast took up a paper which he said was the right date, article in it." So, had the constable moved this piece of evidence, picked it up off the floor and put it into the paper rack and then never mentioned that he had done so? Daniel Chadwick, during re-direct examination, wanted to make sure he heard this surprising setback correctly. Miner answered that he was "under the impression that Tillinghast picked up the paper. Don't know that he took one from the rack." After lengthy objections and counter-objections, Miner still held his ground. "Can't say if it was Tillinghast but think it was," he

---

136 *New London Evening Telegram*, January 22, 1875.

said.[137] It seems that the Borough constable had not only picked up Libby's hat and returned it to him, but had also tampered with other elements of the crime scene. As Tillinghast had said earlier, he was no detective.

ANOTHER QUESTION that had been raised in the trial was the matter of the barking dogs. When Maria and Henry Langworthy reached the farm on the Sunday night of the murder, the dogs were still inside, in the ell behind the kitchen. Libby had not let them out as he usually did after 8 p.m. However, if robbers had broken into the house, and if Libby had "fought them off," wouldn't the dogs have barked loudly? Miss Hattie Gardner was called to the stand on Thursday to tell what she witnessed on Sunday, April 19. She said that she lived near the Langworthys and had been visiting at the Samuel Langworthy home from about 4:30 p.m. until about 8:30. She left Samuel's house and headed north. When she approached the driveway to Henry Langworthy's farm, she explained, "Heard a dog bark. Can't say if more than one dog, but should think more than one. They didn't bark long." Under cross-examination, Miss Gardner reconfirmed her story and added, "The bark was not a very furious one. The dogs did not seem very disturbed." Maria Langworthy had testified that the dogs had barked furiously when she arrived home just after 10 p.m. Surely, if there had been strangers in the house around 8:30, which is when the murder was estimated to have occurred, the dogs would have been very agitated and barking loudly. Hattie Gardner's testimony prompted Constable Tillinghast's return to the witness stand on Friday. He had "neglected" to state previously that Libby told him "a dog barked" just about the time that he was struck over the head. Miss Gardner also noticed that there was no light

---

137 Ibid.

coming from Farmer's Palace, and there "had always been a very bright light there before." [138]

ONE REQUIREMENT of any murder trial is testimony regarding the murder weapon. The prosecution in the Libby trial called upon Dr. Abiel W. Nelson, the New London physician and surgeon who had conducted tests on the iron drill to verify that it was indeed the weapon.[139] Unfortunately, without the advantage of present day science, such as DNA testing, the doctor could not be as specific as the state's attorney would have wished. "I examined the drill and found marks which might have been those of human blood or some other," said Dr. Nelson. "The blood corpuscles are of the proper size to be human being," but it was "not possible to distinguish between stains made by human blood and those made by blood of a dog or brute animal." Under cross-examination, Dr. Nelson explained that he had "measured by use of a microscope and micrometer." "It is delicate work," he said, "but there is no reason for mistakes." Then the doctor introduced an additional problem with the blood on the drill. He could not be sure whether or not the "blood came from being thrown against the clothes." He was referring to the possibility that Courtland's bedding, when it was carried into the woodshed, may have splattered blood on the drill.[140]

As the trial progressed through Thursday and Friday, more details were revealed regarding the bedding and the drill. Evidently, very early on Monday morning, the day after the murder, two

---

138 Ibid.

139 Dr. Nelson's advertisement in the *New London Evening Telegram* read: "A.W. Nelson, M.D., Crocker's Hotel, Room 5, Ladies' Entrance on Union St., Day & Night, 12 M to 2 PM, 5 – 7 PM." Crocker's Hotel (or the Crocker House) still stands on State Street at the corner of Union Street in New London.

140 *New London Evening Telegram*, January 22, 1875.

men, "a colored man named Reed and a man named Crumb," were enlisted to carry Courtland's blood-soaked mattress out of the house.[141] Calvin Sutton, a friend of Hamilton Langworthy, was there to witness this event, and he testified:

> I saw the bed when it came out of the house. It was turned up at the four corners and carried that way into the wood house. There is a work bench on the right hand side of the door as you go in and the iron drill was under that bench. The bed was carried in and placed on a pile of wood. Don't think it possible that the blood stains on the drill could have come from the bed. Saw the blood on sides of the door, of the ell door. I was on the platform of the wagon house. I overtook them within a rod of the wood house and followed them right in. I wanted to see the bed and see how much blood there was on it. Had the bed not been closed up, it would have struck the sides of the door.[142]

William Brewster, a member of the Stonington inquest jury, took the stand and described the scene at the farm a little later that Monday morning in April.

> After going into the house and noticing the remains of Irvin, I first went out to the wood house and noticed there in the right hand corner, an iron drill…Think the wood house fronted south. I saw stains on the drill, but don't claim to know if they were or were not those of blood… the bed clothes lay as they generally would upon being thrown down. The drill stood very near the door. The clothes had

---

141 This information was contained in testimony given by Margaret Brown on Friday, January 22, 1875. It is not known who Reed was, but according to the 1868 map a William Crumb lived on the west side of Quiambog Cove, a few houses north of Captain Miner.

142 *New London Evening Telegram,* January 23, 1875.

been taken in past the door. Can't say if they struck the drill. [Here, Brewster showed the position of the drill, referring to Palmer's diagram.] Usual quantity, the bed clothing was all taken in past that door... The clothes were saturated. Looked as though they were taken in one mass and thrown there. All I am willing to say is it was possible for the clothes to strike the drill, but it is not very reasonable to suppose the drill might be touched with blood and this door not touched. Did not myself notice anything particular about the drill, but picked it up and carried it to the foreman [E. C. Denison].[143]

Brewster was unwilling to allow the defense to imply that the blood on the drill came from the bedclothes. The wood shed doorjamb showed no evidence of blood, and therefore the drill must have already had blood on it before the early morning deposit of the bedclothes.

ONE OF THE PROSECUTION's final witnesses was New London County Sheriff O. N. Raymond. As soon as the sheriff took the stand in order to repeat conversations that he had had with Libby, the defense objected vigorously. The prosecution countered with objections of its own. However, Judge Martin overruled the objections, and Raymond was allowed to continue. He had discussed the case with Libby on Wednesday, April 22, for the first time. Libby had told him that he knew he "was in trouble but thought he would come out all right."

The story Libby told Raymond started out along the same lines as his testimony to the inquest jury. When the sheriff asked about Mr. Langworthy's gun, Libby was unable to account for how the gun turned up in the barn, but related the following story:

---

143 Ibid., January 22, 1875.

I went up west after hay; think it was on Saturday. Mr. Langworthy took his gun along. When we got back he told me to draw the hay and throw if off and he would come out or send Irvin to take care of it. He went down into the orchard with his gun and shot at a crow. [Later, Mr. Langworthy] and Irvin were in the house, at their suppers. I never saw the gun after he went down to shoot crows. I am sure he fired it off, one barrel, as was his habit.

Sheriff Raymond then asked Libby whether he was wearing his cap when he left the house that night. The answer was yes; he had it on at Samuel's. Asked whether he had it on when Tillinghast arrested him, he said, "Yes, or not exactly on. It hurt my head and I laid it down and put my head on it." Raymond thereupon said that Tillinghast had found the hat in the house, and Libby said, "It was a d––d lie." The hat was given to Raymond to examine while he was on the witness stand, and he remarked that there were "cuts in it."[144]

Sheriff Raymond testified that the prisoner had started to elaborate on theories of his own about motives for the murder, attempting to deflect suspicion away from himself and on to others. Raymond said that Libby told him, "No one about there liked Irvin, everybody hated him and a good many had threatened him." Libby even went so far as to say that he thought that the neighbor, Jeffery, and his father might have committed the murder. Jeffery had once threatened to kill him. When Raymond asked Libby what Jeffery had against Irvin, Libby had said that the neighbor had insulted and stoned him and that "he was a very ugly man when drunk." However, Libby noted that he had not seen Jeffery for some time. On the subject of the Langworthys, Raymond said Libby told him that they were "very envi-

---

144 Ibid., January 23, 1875.

ous" and "nobody liked them, that they were not what they pretend to be." He had sometimes listened at the door and heard them talking about him, but when he went inside, they were "very good and had him have enough and of the best to eat." When Raymond asked him what he thought "the object of the murder" could have been, Libby replied, "I have heard of the Langworthy's talking about me behind my back. When I go in, they are honey. Don't know whether they have anything to do with this matter or not, but they are curious folks."[145] This testimony of Raymond's would seem to have undermined the prosecution's indictment of Libby. However, the sheriff was allowed to continue.

At this juncture, Sheriff Raymond stated that he had interviewed Libby again on May 8 in the jail cell in New London. The prisoner had given him "a history of himself since fourteen years of age." (Unfortunately, this history is not included in the testimony.) The sheriff continued, "Libby told me he had something he wished to tell me, but didn't know whether he had better." After hesitating, Raymond, who admitted that he had tried to prevent defense counsel from seeing their client, proceeded to reveal this previously untold and quite startling story.

> In the fall of 1873, while trimming apple trees in the lower orchard, I [Libby] was out on a long limb and Hamilton was on the same limb with his trimming. ...the limb was limber. I said to him, "I think I shall sell my life here." He [Hamilton] said to me, "What would you take for it?" I said, "I don't know." He said if I would waylay his two brothers, put them out of the way, he would give me $300. I laughed at him, thought him joking. Again toward the spring, he and I were down cutting brush part of a day and the next.

---

145 Ibid.

He sat down under a tree to fix our scythes and he then said to me, "Then you don't want to sell your life?" I said to him, "I have had such a good offer I shall have to rise higher." He said, "I will give you $500 if you will way lay the two of them and put them out of the way." I then asked him his object in putting them out of the way. He told me, "Irvin would get all his mother's property and part of his father's and Courtland will get the remainder, leaving me with nothing." I then asked him what he would do with his father and mother, he said they would die shortly. I then laughed at him and he said, "then you don't want the job?" I said, "*No, sir.*" He said, "If you don't want the job somebody else will be glad to get it—times are hard now." He had said occasionally, "You do not want to sell your life then?" He said he would put me under oath to not let a living soul know. Sometime after this Frank Williams was there. I was in the barn picking turkeys. He came in and asked where Hamilton was. Told him he had gone to Noank. He asked where the old man was; I told him, in the house. He asked me how I like working there. I told him, "Very well," then went into the house with the turkeys. He went into the carriage house, stopped in there until Hamilton came home. I and Courtland went for a load of hay and got home about the same time as Hamilton. Williams and Hamilton went into the carriage house and talked for a long time. Hamilton gave him some money and he went away.

In fact, Henry Langworthy had testified the day before that Hamilton had lent Frank Williams some money the week before the murder. On Friday morning, the prosecution was able to call Frank Williams to the stand. Williams stated that he lived in Westerly and had worked for Henry Langworthy for two years, 1872 and 1873. Referring to the money, he said, "I went there [Darling Hill] in February 1874 and had been out of work some time and wanted money and knew I could procure it there. I borrowed $13 from Hamilton. He did not have money enough in his pocket and got enough of his father to make it up." Libby's story about Hamilton paying someone to "way lay" his brothers started to fall apart. Even in 1874, when the country was coping with recession and unemployment, a thirteen-dollar bribe would not have been enough incentive to commit double murder.[146]

BRINGING ITS PHASE of the trial to a close, the prosecution chose the tactic of letting the prisoner be entrapped by his own words. Stiles T. Stanton, clerk of the Stonington inquest jury, was called to the stand to read Libby's answers to questions posed by Edwin B. Trumbull on Monday, April 20, the day after the murder. Whereupon the murder trial's defense counsel raised objections, and Stanton was required to limit his testimony to cover only questions regarding what took place on the night of the murder. Again the trial jury heard how "somebody reached a club" by Libby, clipping him on "the left side of the head in front," smashing the lamp and bludgeoning Irvin. The accused man was hit three times, "once on each temple and once on the back of the head…so quickly I could not tell who did it." Here was the crucial inconsistency of Libby's story. He claimed before the inquest jury, "The first blow knocked me out of the chair. Was struck the second blow on top of the head while I was on the floor. Remember nothing about the third blow." However, the trial jury, no doubt, remembered Samuel Langworthy's testimony stating that Libby had told him he had "fought off robbers as long as he could." Libby had also told Henry Langworthy the same story about fighting off robbers. Stanton continued with Libby's statement about running to Samuel Langworthy's house for help and back up to the barn to tell Henry Langworthy what had hap-

---

146 Ibid.

pened.¹⁴⁷ Libby said he had "followed the carriage up into the horse barn and was too weak to go into the house so laid down on a meal bag." No mention was made of lying down on his hat, and the State rested its case.¹⁴⁸

WHAT NEW EVIDENCE could the defense introduce? What new witness could possibly corroborate the accused man's story of robbers and blows on the head? How to create the reasonable doubt needed to keep William Libby a free man, or at least to keep him from the gallows? Andrew Lippitt made one last effort to prove that Libby had been severely attacked, so severely that blood had collected under his chair in the kitchen. He called Margaret Brown to the stand. Mrs. Brown identified herself as a Stonington resident, living about two miles from the Langworthys' farm, and continued with her account:

> I was never in the house until the day after the murder. Captain Thomas Miner came to my house for me to go there about 5 o'clock Monday morning. I got there about 6 o'clock. I went there to keep Mrs. Langworthy company and take care of the house. I cleaned up the rooms and washed the boy. Some of [Courtland's] clothes I carried out, but the worst had been taken to the sink room in a tub to be washed. There were marks of blood on the casing to the stairway. It looked as though they were made by clothes brushing the walls. Also cleared the kitchen up, most of the blood was near the stove. The carpet near the table was taken up and was out doors near the door step. The blood on the oilcloth was in drops and where it had been tracked.

---

147 Libby stated that when he went to Samuel Langworthy's house for help, he "ran across the three-cornered lot by the wall." That triangular lot and stone wall are still visible today along Lord's Hill Road.

148 *New London Evening Telegram,* January 23, 1875.

> There were drops of blood on the door near the sink back of where Irvin sat. There was blood on the floor between the table and the stove. It was 7 and 8 o'clock in the morning when I washed up the blood.

This testimony was not helping Libby's case. If anything, it made plain the fact that the pool of blood was only under Irvin's chair, and evidence of blood around the house could have been made by Libby's clothes or shoes as well as anyone else's. In cross-examination, Attorney Chadwick questioned Mrs. Brown about a new bit of evidence. "Did you see the shirt of Libby that morning?" he asked. The neighbor replied that she "saw a blue navy shirt on the arbor that morning but did not know who it belonged to, and no one knew how it came to be washed." The defense objected to this line of questioning as the evidence had not been "touched upon" in direct examination. Chadwick claimed that it was "admissible on the ground that [Margaret Brown] had been called upon to testify as to the condition of things generally at the house on the morning after the murder." Since that morning in April, Mrs. Brown had learned that the navy-issue shirt belonged to Libby. Had Libby tried to wash blood evidence off his shirt on Sunday evening before he ran to Samuel Langworthy's for help? This proposition was difficult to determine as it was pouring rain early Monday morning, and everything left outside would have been soaking wet.[149]

THE DEFENSE ATTORNEYS tried another tactic. Neighbors had reported seeing strangers in the area the night of April 19, and each of these strangers could be considered a potential suspect. Prosecutor Daniel Chadwick had already interrogated James Coleman, who identified himself as the man in the road with a

---

149 Ibid. Margaret Brown may have been related to W. M. Brown who lived on the east side of Cove Road, north of Captain Miner.

white coat. "This, Mr. Lippitt, is the white coated gentleman," Chadwick had announced, daring the frustrated defense attorney to pursue that tired story. However, there were other unidentified men travelling the Quiambog district on the night of the murder. The defense attorney must have hoped that the following witnesses' statements would create enough doubt to help Libby's case. Of course, in 1874, with no telephone and no automobiles, it would have been common enough to find messengers, neighbors, and other locals using the roads and paths. Today, these accounts inform our understanding of nineteenth-century rural existence, specifically in one section of Stonington. But, for the purposes of the trial, such testimony was needed to reinforce the shroud of mystery that defense counsel, as well as newspaper reporters, relied on to envelop the case.

Henry B. Austin was the first of these witnesses to take the stand. He said he lived in on the west side of Quiambog Cove along the north-south road, meaning what we now call Cove Road. "Have lived in the neighborhood about twenty years," he explained. "My business is working around by day or month at what I can get to do." Austin carefully described the upper Quiambog area.

> There is a stone quarry about 20 rods northward from the school house on the main [Cove] road. There is a roadway that runs down by Langworthy's and comes out near Samuel Langworthy's. There is a dwelling house near the schoolhouse on the west side of the old road which belongs to Jesse Miner. There are two buildings on this road. The other belongs to Kelly, and is on the opposite side of the road from Miner's and nearer Langworthy's and is 30 rods I should say from the schoolhouse. There is a bridgeway across the cove near the schoolhouse. Only other bridge

is near Captain Miner's. No other way of crossing the cove.[150]

The defense counselor asked Henry Austin what he remembered about the night of the murder. The man then proceeded with his well-rehearsed recollection:

> I was at [Randall] Brown's, which is a north course from the quarry. Went there to pay him some money. Left there to go home about nine o'clock. I sat 15 or 20 minutes after that—perhaps half an hour. I went along till I got betwixt the quarry and schoolhouse when I heard something. It sounded to me like a man or a critter running to the eastward off to my left. I stopped and listened twice and each time I heard it again. I stepped up to the wall and looked over and there lay some sheep. While I stood there I heard the noise again. I thought to myself I will go down to the schoolhouse and make a stop. I went there and stopped on the north side. Hadn't been there a second when a man came along down the road that leads from Langworthy's and run up into the main road about 18 to 20 feet from me and then went right across the road over a pair of bars [a gate] and up the hill. Where he went over the bars is a cross road from Stonington to Mystic cutting off three or four miles. He kept on a sharp run as far as I could see him. He had a low wide-brimmed hat and dark coat. Never

---

150 Ibid. The roadway Austin was describing is a pentway, which heads downhill from Cove Road opposite the Jesse Miner (presently the David M. Rathbun) house. The Quiambog District schoolhouse stood on the north side of this intersection. The pentway continued east over the cove, as Austin described, and connected with another pentway running south along the east bank of Quiambog Cove. Today, most of this pentway is called Wilbur Road. In 1874, it ended near Samuel Langworthy's and joined the main road coming up from the "new bridge" near Thomas Miner's. In September 1867, Henry Langworthy sold property (see 1868 Beers map) he owned on the northern end of this pentway to John and Mary Kelly.

saw him before. He was middling-sized, nothing remarkable about the man. When I first heard him I think he must have been near Kelly's house. The night was still and neither very light nor dark. From where I saw the man to Mr. Langworthy's house I should think was about half a mile. Next morning one of my neighbors, Mr. Wilcox, came into my house about sunrise and asked me if I had heard that all the folks in the house on the hill were murdered the night before and the fact makes me recollect particularly where I was on the night before the murder.[151]

Under cross-examination, Austin admitted that he had not actually seen the man come from the direction of the Langworthy's, but only assumed so after hearing about the murder.

THE DEFENSE NEXT called Oliver Denison to attest to the peaceful scene on Darling Hill early on that fateful Sunday evening. Denison, who lived "about three-quarters of a mile from the school house in a northwest course," said he was at Farmer's Palace around 6 p.m. "Had some cider. It was drawn for me—perhaps a quart of it—I drank only a single glass of it. Saw nobody else drink any." Denison reported that Libby and Courtland were in and out of the barn, tending to the evening's routine chores. However, when Attorney Chadwick asked Denison what he knew about the man seen by Austin, he replied, "I heard about a man running over the drift road that night, but know nothing about it personally. If a man from Mr. Crandall's was going for a doctor from Mystic, he would go by this road." Apparently, Mrs. Crandall, who lived on the pentway below the Langworthys' (Wilbur Road), was in need of a doctor that Sunday night.

Another Quiambog resident had seen an unidentified man that

---

151 *New London Evening Telegram*, January 23, 1875.

Sunday night also. Joseph Cavanaugh recollected the night of the murder, April 19:[152]

> I was at Robert Jeffery's, on the other side of the cove opposite my house. Jeffery's place is northwest from Langworthy's about a quarter of a mile [1868 map shows R. P. Jeffery's house on the east side of the cove next to Crandall]. I went across the cove to Jeffery's in a boat and got there about 7:30 or a little after. Landed abreast of Jeffery's house. When I went ashore, thought I saw a man east from me and below me. He was standing there. I did not know him, but took him to be Mr. Jeffery. I went immediately to Jeffery's house and found him there by the stove with his shoes off, smoking. Then went outdoors and looked around with Mr. Jeffery to look up the man I had seen. The man was about five feet, ten inches I should judge with dark sack coat and black slouched hat… Jeffery and I were outdoors about ten minutes. From where I saw him towards Langworthy's house there is a piece of juniper and there is a wall running up the hill to Langworthy's house. From the time I landed till Jeffery and I went out was not more than two minutes.[153]

When questioned by the prosecution, Cavanaugh said that he had been unable to tell which direction the man had come from or where he disappeared to, only that he had been about 10 rods (165 feet) away. Was this the same man seen by Austin coming from the pentway and crossing the road?

---

152 The Cavanaugh house is situated near the bend on Cove Road, between the road and the cove. According to Wheeler, it was built in 1770 by William Miner, and was distinguished by "the well with the old oaken bucket hanging from the sweep" in the front yard. *Homes of Our Ancestors*, pp. 61-62.

153 *New London Evening Telegram*, January 23, 1875.

Libby's defense team was able to come up with a suspicious stranger as far away as North Stonington. Welcome H. Geer, who lived on the George C. Brown farm "in the south part of the town, on the line between that town and Stonington, on the road from Mystic to Milltown (North Stonington village), was sworn in and asked to tell about the man he met on Monday morning.

> Have lived there eight years and am a farmer. Was at Mr. Brown's the day after the murder, all day. First I heard of the murder a young man came along the road going to Milltown and I was in the lot. He asked me if I heard the accident the night before. He then went on to tell that he came from Providence that morning. (Here the attorney for the state objected to this testimony as of a hearsay character and was argued at length by counsel. The court held that the testimony was inadmissable.) I was in a lot, west of the road, within 6 feet of the road. The man I saw was a tall, slim young man with dark hair and eyes and smooth face. I should recognize him if I saw him. Saw a mark in India ink around his wrist in blue and red, supposed it to be meant for a wreath. Think he had on a light sack coat and dark pantaloons. He had a handkerchief around his neck, with his collar open. Had a striped cotton shirt in his hand, wrapped in a paper. When I first saw him, he was between the bars and the house. He spoke to me first. We were both at the bars at the time. It was raining at this time. Had no knowledge of this murder before I got it from this man. He told me there had been a murder. Never saw the man before and never since. Talked with him fifteen minutes. He went on towards Milltown.[154]

---

154 Ibid. Although the *Telegram* reported that the court found this testimony "inadmissable," the testimony was reported in the press.

Geer confirmed that the man was "coming from the south and going northwest." Therefore, the stranger came from the Stonington direction. If he had come from Providence that morning, it seems that he must have come by train or boat, and he certainly would have heard talk of the murder at the Stonington train station or pier.

UP TO THIS POINT in the trial, William Libby's defense attorneys had attempted to prove that his account of the night of April 19 could possibly be accurate. The barking dogs, the hat, the newspaper, the gun, the door knobs, the man's own wounds—these details were all addressed, however shakily. Strangers seen in the neighborhood presented the possibility that the story about robbers might just be true, despite the fact that none of these strangers appeared very sinister. Nevertheless, Andrew Lippitt and Charles Butler seemed to realize that Libby, himself, would not be able to take the stand and successfully fend off rigorous questioning from Daniel Chadwick or John Wait. The *New London Evening Telegram*, always eager for more sensational courtroom material, held out hope until the proceedings were "unexpectedly brought to a close at 1:30 p.m." on Friday, January 23, after only two and a half days of testimony. Speaking of the defense attorneys, the *Telegram* wrote, "Their failure to put the prisoner on the stand was a great disappointment to the spectators who crowded the Court Room."[155]

THE ATTORNEYS' concluding arguments in the Libby trial began at 10:30 a.m. on Monday, January 25, and they attracted a large crowd. The *New London Evening Telegram* reported that "several hundred persons gathered in front of the court house, but ad-

---

155 Ibid., January 22, 1875.

mission was denied until after the arrival of the judges by the 11 o'clock train from Norwich." When the proceedings began, "seats reserved for spectators were all full [and] large numbers were unable to gain admittance."

COLONEL JOHN T. WAIT delivered the first closing argument for the prosecution. This sixty-three-year-old former Speaker of the Connecticut House of Representatives had lost his own son a dozen years earlier at the Battle of Antietam, and he spoke with considerable empathy, as well as a touch of drama. "The parents of the lad had left him at an early hour upon that evening in the full enjoyment health and life. On their return to that home some few hours later they found the lifeless body of their son reclining in a chair, his inanimate form already cold and stiffened with the chill of death and the floor of their dwelling red with his blood." The case, Wait pointed out, was based entirely on circumstantial evidence since there were no eyewitnesses. But, he added, "many little circumstances connected together bind the criminal with crime with a chain too strong for professional skill or telling eloquence to sunder."[156]

Colonel Wait then turned his focus onto the prisoner, William Libby. The hired man was the "one single person" who was intimately acquainted with the premises on Darling Hill and who had threatened the victim. The fact that Libby had tried to incriminate Hamilton Langworthy only demonstrated his desperation. During the trial, several instances had been described which repeatedly showed Libby's dislike of the family. Wait hinted that Libby's past had a "prior blemish," but the prosecution was "not permitted to impart that knowledge." In a blatant play on class differences, Wait stated, "A trivial motive would be more apt to

---

156 *New London Evening Telegram*, January 25, 1875.

influence a man of Libby's standing, limited education and mode of life than it would a man in a high social position."¹⁵⁷

As the counselor went on to list the circumstantial evidence, the attention of people in the courtroom suddenly shifted to the prisoner's dock. "Intense excitement prevailed in the room in consequence of the fainting of the prisoner. He had been deadly pale for some minutes and now dropped like a dead man against the side of the dock with his countenance rigid and ghastly. The sheriff bathed his head with cold water, the window near him was opened and in a few minutes he recovered though still deadly pale."¹⁵⁸ Was it Wait's powerful argument or a lack of proper nourishment and medical care in the jail that caused the weakened Libby to faint? We can only surmise that the bleakness of his situation was taking a toll on the prisoner. However, Colonel Wait was not deterred by this disturbance. He continued with his analysis of the evidence, ironically remarking that it was "improbable that outsiders would have passed by Libby" as he was such a "stout and powerful" man. In all, John Wait's argument lasted three hours.¹⁵⁹

DEFENSE COUNSEL Charles Butler followed the prosecution, presenting his closing argument on Monday afternoon. Butler sought to evoke the jury's sympathy for the prisoner, "that man who sits here hour after hour, day after day, a silent and helpless spectator of the struggle. He sits alone in the midst of this gazing multitude, a stranger, [seeing] not one countenance of kinsman or friend." Butler turned the class issue around. "It is not enough that the rights of the wealthy and the influential are cared for,"

---

157   Ibid.
158   *Mystic Press,* January 29, 1875.
159   *New London Evening Telegram,* January 25, 1875.

he said. The jury must be mindful of "the rights of the poorest and humblest stranger." And he warned of the harm that would be done, "if through prejudice or bias or neglect or indifference, you should do to this prisoner, who is in your hands, any injustice." Butler was still concerned that Libby had been arrested and jailed before the Stonington inquest jury had delivered its verdict. Moving on to the evidence brought out in the trial, he dismissed each point as "improbable," "exaggerated," or "uncertain." Furthermore, Courtland Langworthy's testimony should be disregarded, as Courtland proved "not a credible witness and his bodily and mental vision were so impaired that he could neither accurately observe nor reliably narrate events." Concluding his three hour argument, Butler tried to emphasize that no motive had been proved, the motive of ill feeling being "an indignity to the intelligence of the jury."[160]

ON TUESDAY MORNING, January 26, State's Attorney Daniel Chadwick stood before the jury to present his summation of the case. He reviewed all the pertinent circumstances and evidence, dwelling on the importance of the cap found upstairs. He demonstrated that Libby was sitting in a chair facing the stove and "the explanation as to the moving of the chair by Mrs. Langworthy's dress sweeping against it is absurd." "Circumstantial evidence is a combination of facts," Chadwick stated, "as the hawser is composed of a number of strands." The most puzzling question raised by Libby's story was how intruders could bludgeon both Langworthys and only graze Libby's head. There was no evidence of a struggle. "Isn't this the most wonderful thing in the world?" Chadwick questioned how the intruders could have possibly gotten past the tall and heavyset Libby, who, having now lost much of his weight, sat stonily in the prisoner's dock.

---

160 Ibid.

"Did he fight with them, as he said, or did he get knocked insensible?" The two contradicting stories completely undermined Libby's testimony. The State's Attorney then addressed the accusation that Hamilton Langworthy had instigated the attacks on his brothers. Contradiction of Libby's account would have to be made "outside of court." Hamilton's testimony was inadmissable as he had not been anywhere near Darling Hill on the night of the murder. However, Chadwick said, pointing toward Libby, "The man who could assassinate the character of the living son, could have been the assassin of the dead boy."[161]

DEFENSE COUNSEL Andrew C. Lippitt presented the final closing argument on Tuesday afternoon. He went over the details of the case again, finding reasons to doubt the testimony of the prosecution witnesses. Mr. Langworthy, he said, seemed to have been a bit deaf. He claimed that Langworthy had heard Libby say, "I have fought them off," when actually the exact words were, "I have done all I could." The defense attorney ignored the issue of the locked doors. According to Lippitt, the weakest testimony came from Constable Samuel K. Tillinghast. In describing the scene at the farm, the defense counsel said, "Mr. Tillinghast is too careless in making his statements and leaves out things." The prosecution had dwelt on the evidence of the cap found in the upstairs hall, but several people had been in that hall and had not seen the cap. Lippitt, dismissing the cap evidence, declared that Tillinghast's "zeal carries him beyond his knowledge."

With this remark, Lippitt himself proceeded beyond his own knowledge. He took the time to create an elaborate scenario of several robbers entering the house, overpowering Libby, and brandishing Henry Langworthy's gun. Finally, Lippitt referred

---

161 Ibid., January 26, 1875.

to Daniel Chadwick's earlier simile comparing the collection of evidence to a hawser. "The attempt to make the rope," he said, "has failed in all its strands—a rope to hang Libby."[162]

ANDREW LIPPITT's closing argument was so lengthy that it was continued from Tuesday into Wednesday morning. That afternoon, Chief Justice John D. Park delivered the charge to the jury. His prime concern appeared to be insuring that the jury understood the distinction between murder in the first degree and murder in the second degree. For a first-degree murder conviction, the decision had to be based upon the expression of malice aforethought as well as the testimony of two witnesses. Murder in the second degree required only implied malice. While the State had claimed a motive of malice, motive did not have to be definitively proven as long as there was ample evidence. Park concluded his charge reminding the jury of their duty, "justice to the memory of the dead and to the bereaved relatives of the deceased, and to the prisoner at the bar charged with this great and awful crime."[163] At 3:40 p.m. on Wednesday, January 27, the jury retired to conduct its deliberations.

AT 5:20 P.M., LESS THAN two hours later but too late for any kind of write-up in the evening newspapers, the Libby jury returned to the courtroom, ready to deliver its verdict. A number of spectators were on hand, as Foreman William L. Peckham stepped forward and read aloud, "Guilty of murder in the second degree." The *Evening Telegram* reported in Thursday's edition that "the silence for an instance remained unbroken, so great the surprise." All eyes shifted to William Libby. "An instant change

---

162 Ibid., January 27, 1875.
163 Ibid.

in the demeanor of the prisoner was evident to all who noticed him. He looked more cheerful than before and apparently was content with the result. He had been under the very shadow of the gallows." Evidently, Libby had expected "to pay the penalty of his awful crime with his life." The newspaper divulged that Libby indeed had narrowly escaped the gallows. The jury's first vote was five in favor of murder in the first degree, four in favor of the second-degree, and three for acquittal. A compromise was subsequently agreed on with all in favor of the sentence of murder in the second degree, and Chief Justice John Park remanded Libby to jail to await sentencing.

Thursday's editorial in the *New London Evening Telegram* was devoted to the Libby trial, which, Tibbits noted, was "conducted with marked ability." He remarked that the arguments on both sides were "devoid of all attempts at rhetorical flourish," although that claim could certainly be argued. Unwilling to give up the overriding popular theme of the case, Tibbits added, "The fact that the claim rested solely on circumstantial evidence served to invest the case with an air of MYSTERY."[164]

JUST BEFORE NOON on Friday, January 29, William Libby was brought into the courtroom in New London, placed in the prisoner's dock, and ordered to stand. Judge Earl Martin, who had presided over the trial, was ready to pronounce sentence. He prefaced the sentencing, however, with a withering address to the prisoner. Libby, Martin said, was not only guilty of "the willful and malicious murder of Irvin Langworthy," but guilty of complete and utter ingratitude as well. Again, we encounter the notion that the Langworthys had somehow anointed William Libby with the status of family member. Of course, in keeping

---

164 Ibid., January 28, 1875.

with nineteenth-century values, the sanctity of family was paramount, and Libby had violated it. He was a "servant," who had the opportunity to improve his status, to take his place as part of the Langworthy family, if only he had been obedient and acted appreciatively. Martin's address is remarkable for its depth of emotion and accomplished literary style.

> You had been a member of the family whose happiness you destroyed. Day after day you toiled side by side with your victim in the field and met with him around the family board, and when at night you rested from your toil, under the same roof with him you sought repose. You were treated more like a son than a servant. But when the parents of that innocent and beloved boy left him to your protection while they went to the house of worship in the darkness and stillness of the night while he, in the indulgence of his passion for knowledge, was poring over his book, you stole behind him and with upraised bludgeon inflicted upon him a blow that instantly deprived him of life and sent him without a moment's warning into the presence of his Maker. Not satisfied with the deed, marked as it was with both cruelty and cowardice, you wended your tortuous way to the room where night after night you and the murdered man and another had slept in fancied security and there inflicted murderous wounds upon one whose physical infirmities should have been his protection. Not satisfied with this feast of blood—the carnival of cruelty— you sought by false charges to cast the burden of your guilt upon another and to cause an innocent person to expiate on the gallows the crime which you had committed. You were there in the confidence of the father and the mother. They left in your care their jewels—the son in whose future career of usefulness and honor they had the brightest

hopes. You basely betrayed their confidence. You violated hospitality.[165]

According to Judge Martin's interpretation, Libby was not just hired for his ability as a sturdy farmhand; he had been invited into Farmer's Palace as a family member as well as a caretaker of the family. From his own statements, it is not at all clear that Libby had seen himself in this role. Was he to be included in this family? Regardless of whether the story about Hamilton's offer was true, it does illustrate the fact that Libby realized the Langworthy sons would inherit property. Whether the Langworthy sons worked hard or not, they would ultimately end up with property, and he understood that he would not.

Judge Martin went on to deliver a mixed message regarding the condemned man's future. Although the jury had found Libby guilty, they had "tempered justice with the divine attribute of mercy." While in prison, Libby should set about reforming his life.

> If your thoughts in the silent confinement to which you go do not awaken in your heart and conscience a feeling of remorse, no words of mine can avail to do it. But you can not call back from the remorseless grave the dead form, or bring to life the hopes and aspirations that there lie buried. The deed is irrevocable and beyond reparation. You can not restore to the fond father and the doting mother the darling child. But this you may do—in the life that is yet continued to you, you may show evidences of penitence and contrition. Bad as your life has been, it is in your power to make it better. It is to be hoped that you may improve this solemn lesson, life-lasting in its effects.

---

165 Ibid., January 29, 1875.

However, the life that the judge portrayed was more than bleak. Libby was going to be "permitted to live but to live within the walls of a dungeon removed from all joys of existence, from home, from friends, from society, dragging out as it were a living death."[166]

Finally, Judge Martin sentenced the twenty-one-year-old William Libby to life imprisonment at the Connecticut State Prison in Wethersfield. Again, a reporter was in the courtroom to record the scene. "While sentence was being pronounced upon him, [Libby] manifested considerable emotion and from the deathly pallor that spread over his countenance, it was feared that he might be attacked with a fainting turn similar to that by which he was overcome during the argument of the case."[167]

THE LEWISTON, MAINE, *Evening Journal*, which had been carrying news of the trial, stated on Monday, February 1, "The Libby just convicted of murder in Connecticut is a native of Webster, and his father now resides in Sabattus. The convicted man two or three years since escaped from the hands of officers in this city and now turns up in the last extremity of crime."[168] Had they read this bit of information, the Langworthys might well have been dismayed to discover that the man they invited into their home had already had a run-in with the law. It seems that Libby may have "escaped" from the Lewiston police by enlisting in the Navy in 1872 at the age of eighteen. Despite the *Evening Journal*'s report, however, the reputation of the greater part of the Libby family in Maine continued to remain sterling. A 1909 history described Libbys as "generally belong[ing] to that law abiding class

---

166 Ibid.
167 Ibid.
168 Lewiston, Maine, *Evening Journal*, February 1, 1875.

• **The Trial**

[handwritten annotation: "that class of Americans) – CITIZEN"]

which forms the bone and muscle of the nation," mostly businessmen, attorneys, and bankers. "Very few have been guilty of bringing any reproach upon the name," and, the book claimed, "a criminal named Libby" had never been known. Perhaps in Maine this statement was true, but not in Connecticut.[169]

ON TUESDAY, February 2, a warrant of commitment was signed by Webster Park, assistant clerk of the New London Superior Court. And on Wednesday Libby was escorted by a deputy warden on to the 11:15 a.m. train and taken to Wethersfield via the Shore Line and Connecticut Valley Railroad. The warrant commanded the prison warden, E. B. Hewes, to receive the said William B. Libby and "safely keep him at hard labor within State Prison for and during his natural life." The document added that the convicted murderer's labor was intended to repay the State for the cost of prosecution, $748.38.[170]

While a great deal had been made of the fact that Libby received a life sentence rather than hanging, life in prison in the 1870s was tantamount to a death sentence. The Connecticut State Prison in Wethersfield opened in 1827, taking the place of the more primitive Newgate Prison in Granby. However, medical care, especially preventive, was nearly non-existent, and disease frequently shortened a prisoner's "natural life." Wethersfield vital records list prisoners' deaths caused by a variety of communicable diseases, including typhoid, pneumonia, consumption (tuberculosis), and dysentery. The 1882 Libby family genealogy simply lists William B. Libby as having died in Wethersfield,

---

169 George Thomas Little, ed., *Genealogical and Family History of the State of Maine*, 4 vols. (New York: Lewis Historical Publishing Company), p. 307.

170 Department of Corrections Warrants of Commitment 1874-1875, RG 017, Connecticut State Library. *New London Evening Telegram*, February 3, 1875.

Connecticut. Thus, we can surmise that the murderer of Irvin Langworthy, imprisoned at the age of twenty-one, lived only another six or seven years.[171]

The *Mystic Press* reported that Libby's life sentence "was received with a degree of satisfaction by the people of the region." Since the weekly paper was published each Friday, the editor's first opportunity to comment on the outcome of the trial was in the February 5 issue. However, the Mystic paper had more important business to address that Friday. The startling insinuation that Hamilton Langworthy had encouraged the attacks on his brothers needed to be refuted. "The Mystic correspondent of the *Norwich Bulletin* thus defends the character of J. Hamilton Langworthy from the suspicion attempted by William Libby," the story began. Apparently, the Mystic man had been Hamilton's teacher and knew him from childhood. Hamilton, he said, had a "good nature and pleasant temper, was given to frolic and fun, but without lasting resentment. He was and is without malice and would soon forgive and forget an injury." The former teacher asserted that it was impossible that Hamilton would have proposed "such a plot." Furthermore, his "moral and religious principles utterly forbid complicity." The *Mystic Press* ended by denouncing William Libby for his "black conduct to attempt to fasten guilt upon an innocent young man."[172] Throughout the long ordeal caused by Libby's attacks, the Langworthys had repeatedly had their reputations impugned. This defense of Hamilton's character was a final attempt to close the case and clear the family's name for good.

---

171 Connecticut Department of Correction Facilities, www.doc.state.ct.us.gov. Town of Wethersfield Vital Records, Connecticut State Library. A search of these records indicates that the town started recording prisoner deaths only in the mid-1880s. As Libby must have died before 1882, his name was not found. Charles T. Libby, *The Libby Family in America, 1692-1881* (Portland, Maine: Quintin Publications, 1882), p. 516.

172 *The Mystic Press*, February 5, 1875.

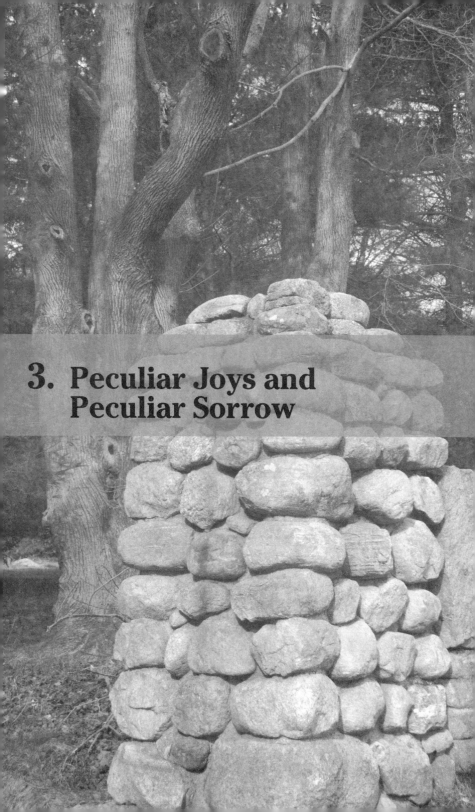

3. Peculiar Joys and Peculiar Sorrow

After the exhausting tension of the Libby trial, the Langworthys returned to their routine on Darling Hill in Stonington. They sought to reclaim the peace and safety of Farmer's Palace, which had been so threatened by the savage murder and assault. At the same time, the Langworthy family found themselves living in a period of unprecedented change. The "Gilded Age," named only two years before in a novel by Mark Twain and Charles Dudley Warner, was in full gear, bringing industrialists, financiers, and speculators to the fore.[173] To compete in this new economy, small farmers, even to hold their own, needed to change their old ways of doing business.

The Darling Hill farm, more than 170 acres, had only twenty cows, give or take one, as Courtland had mentioned during the trial. Henry Langworthy sold milk in Stonington Borough at eight cents a quart. Even had he charged the ten cents that his competition did, the profits from this enterprise could not have supported the farm in the years to come.[174] Of course, Henry

---

173 *The Gilded Age*, by Mark Twain and Charles Dudley Warner, was published in Hartford in 1873. It was Twain's first novel.
174 *The Mystic Press*, January 14, 1875.

and Maria Langworthy owned real-estate investments in the Borough, and the family was able to derive some income from these properties. But in the final quarter of the nineteenth century, as Hamilton Langworthy took his place as head of the family, it became even clearer that change would be inevitable.

On January 11, 1881, almost six years after the Libby trial, Hamilton Langworthy married Hannah Bell Briggs. He was thirty-five years old and was apparently managing the Darling Hill farm for his seventy-one-year-old father. It is not known how Hamilton met Hannah. She was born in Charlestown, Rhode Island, in 1860, and her family lived in the Quonochontaug area. However, Hannah was related to Virginia Briggs, who lived on Farmholme Road in Stonington and taught at the little District 10 schoolhouse in Wequetequock.[175]

Three years after Hamilton and Hannah were married, they had a son, but tragedy soon revisited the family on Darling Hill. The baby, named Irving for his late uncle, died of convulsions on March 12, 1886, at the age of two. Hannah was pregnant at the time and five days later gave birth to a daughter, who was named Maria Pierce for her grandmother.[176] In June, Hannah wrote to her friend, Dora Hoxie, that she thought she would "never get over" little Irving's death. Further, since the birth of baby Maria, she had been coughing and "was thin as a shad." She had consulted Dr. Charles Maine, in Stonington Borough, who referred her to a doctor in New London for treatments and medication

---

175 *Biographical Review*, p. 442. Phyllis Wheeler Grills, *Kith, Kin and Cooks* (1989), p. 405. Virginia Briggs led the 1883 "Wequetequock War," the storming of the schoolhouse, at the intersection of what is now Route 1 and Farmholme Road, by a group of local women who wanted religious services to be held in the building.

176 Town of Stonington Records of Births, Marriages, and Deaths, 1880-1901.

for her lungs. Little Maria, she wrote, was the "worst baby to take care of"—she cried incessantly, and she and Hamilton could barely get any sleep. Hannah wrote her friend that, if she could find a girl to come care for the baby, she would like to get away to Quonochontaug for a few weeks' rest cure. Whether Hannah ever got to Rhode Island is unknown, but the visits to the doctor in New London were in vain. She was unable to regain her health, and she died of consumption on June 23, 1887.[177] The forty-three-year-old Hamilton Langworthy was left a widower with a one-year-old child, who came to be known as Marie.

MEANWHILE, RECORDS SHOW, the senior Langworthys looked increasingly to investments in real estate to bolster their income. In 1877, Maria Langworthy purchased land on Church Street in Stonington Borough. The lot, a fifth of an acre, cost $600. Four years later, the Langworthys sold this same lot for $1,000 to the Borough of Stonington for the construction of a new hall. The handsome three-story building housed the Neptune as well as the Hook and Ladder fire companies on the first floor and had an auditorium with a stage on the second floor. There was also space for Borough offices and a new lock-up.[178] In 1887, Maria

---

177 Hannah B. Langworthy to Dora Hoxie, June 20, 1886, courtesy of Susan Hart. Dr. Charles O. Maine (1843-1916), a physician in Stonington Borough, was a graduate of Dartmouth College. He lived on the corner of Water and Harmony streets and his advertisement in the *Stonington Mirror* claimed that he specialized in lung diseases. The records of Irving's and Hannah's deaths lists Dr. Maine as the Langworthy family physician. Although family sources, including the Langworthy gravestone, and the *Stonington Mirror* list Hannah's death as June 23, 1887, the Town of Stonington of Births, Marriages, and Deaths, 1880-1901, lists it as June 28, 1888.

178 Town of Stonington Land Records, vol. 36, p. 167; vol. 36, p. 544. The new Borough Hall opened in November 1882 (600 people attended the dedication) and was torn down in 1948 to make way for the present hall and firehouse. Haynes, *Stonington Chronology*, p. 98 (picture).

Langworthy purchased a lot and two buildings on the west side of School Street in the lower Borough from the estate of Mrs. Almira Hancox. This property cost Maria $1,825. Presumably she was able to collect rent on the houses.[179] Henry Langworthy began to sell small parcels of the Darling Hill property along Quiambog Cove, the first in 1875 to Joseph Wilbur, one acre for $200. In 1880, Henry sold one and a half acres to William Wilbur's wife, Jane, and he sold her two more acres in 1881, all along Quiambog Cove, receiving a total of $400.[180]

By 1889, Henry Langworthy had ended his forty-year routine of delivering milk in the Borough. Close to eighty years old, he became ill and died at his beloved Darling Hill farm on March 8. The Reverend G. H. Miner of Mystic's Union Baptist Church, assisted by the Reverend Albert G. Palmer, pastor of the First Baptist Church in the Borough, conducted Henry's funeral. The *Mystic Press* printed a tribute to him from an unidentified friend:

> Mr. Langworthy never recovered from the shock occasioned by the murder of his son Irving, by the tramp Libby, some years ago. Perhaps Mr. Langworthy had no more intimate friend than your correspondent, and no friend who understands him better. He was a man of strong convictions and ever ready to give a reason for the faith which he had. We have never seen a man who prized his friends more, who was more grateful for favors conferred, who remembered favors longer, or who could be more unselfish in his friendship. He could differ with his friends in politics, religion, and other exciting topics, and still be a kind courteous host, a reliable friend, and a pleasant neighbor.[181]

---

179 Town of Stonington Land Records, vol. 41, p. 162.
180 Ibid., vol. 35, p. 246; vol. 36, pp. 432, 593.
181 *Mystic Press*, March 14, 1889; *Stonington Mirror*, March 16, 1889.

The paper also noted that "Mrs. Langworthy had had deep sorrow in her family"—the murder of her son, the death of her daughter-in-law, and now the loss of her husband. The reporter did not note that Maria had suffered another recent loss. Her twin sister, Mary Clarke, who lived in Westerly, had arisen early on the morning of May 9, 1888, and was going downstairs to begin an especially busy day. Suddenly, she screamed, "Oh, my head!" and collapsed. The doctor was called but was only able to pronounce Mary dead of apoplexy, a brain hemorrhage.[182]

Henry D. Langworthy's will, which had been drawn up in 1880, carefully portioned out his estate. His wife, Maria, and son Hamilton were named co-executors, but the prime concern in the document seems to have been the welfare of his oldest son, Courtland. Henry stipulated that a sum of $100 be paid annually for Courtland's support "during the term of his natural life." The will left Maria "one-third of all [of Henry's] estate, real and personal, wherever she may be situated, provided she shall pay annually her proportioned part" of Courtland's support. Similarly, Hamilton was left two-thirds of Henry's estate but only if he paid two-thirds of Courtland's annual support. This bequest must have been uppermost in Henry's mind, as it was restated four times in his will. With physical limitations, including vision problems, and with no real estate to his name, Courtland would always need some sort of support, and perhaps Henry understood that Courtland would not continue to live at Hamilton's Farmer's Palace. A codicil to the will left all of Henry's "household goods and furniture of whatever kind" to his widow.[183]

---

182 *Narragansett Weekly*, May 10, 1888.
183 Town of Stonington Probate Records, vol. 26, p. 573. Henry D. Langworthy's will was witnessed by three Mystic men: John Heath, who became vice president of Mystic Industrial Co., manufacturers of velvet in the Greenmanville section; Allen Avery, owner of Allen Avery & Co., a furniture store in Mystic; and John G. Packer. Haynes, *Stonington Chronology*, pp. 87, 89.

At the time of Irvin Langworthy's murder in 1874, the newspapers repeatedly referred to the whole affair as a "mystery." However, what happened on Darling Hill after Henry D. Langworthy's death is perhaps far more of a mystery from today's perspective. What we do know is that Maria Langworthy and her son Hamilton appeared before the Stonington town clerk to sign an agreement in March 1891. Maria leased her one-third of the Darling Hill farm to Hamilton for "an annual rent of $150, payable quarterly." She agreed to pay her share of all repairs and taxes but would cancel the lease if the premises were not kept in good condition or if the rent were more than fifteen days late.[184] Judging from these terms, we might surmise that Maria voluntarily decided to leave Darling Hill, one explanation being that the farm held too many sad memories. On the other hand, the possibility exists that some disagreement with Hamilton precipitated Maria's departure. And Courtland, dependent upon his mother, would leave with her. Thus Hamilton, it seems, stayed on at Farmer's Palace quite alone. It is not certain whether little Marie lived with her father, but more likely she went to live with relatives in Rhode Island. Nor have records been found to document who worked on the farm and whether or not they lived in the house with Hamilton.

After residing on Darling Hill for more than fifty years, Maria Langworthy decamped and moved, with her oldest son Courtland, to West Main Street in Mystic, just down the hill from the Union Baptist Church. She took rooms in what was called the Ketchum Block, the building at 34 West Main Street owned by Rollin S. Ketchum.[185] Maria had not been living in Mystic long

---

184 Town of Stonington Land Records, vol. 44, p. 152.
185 Town of Groton Probate Records, vol. 10, pp. 361, 426. Rollin S. Ketchum bought 34 West Main in 1866 and ran an ice cream saloon on the premises. In 1892, Mrs. Sarah L. Ketchum was the landlady at 34 West Main Street, but the Ketchum family lived on Pearl Street. The building was doubled in size in 1911, and today it is the location of a restaurant. Mystic River Historical Society.

before she met with a tragic as well as ironic demise, described in the *Mystic Press* of April 21, 1892:

> Mrs. Maria Pierce Langworthy, widow of Henry D. Langworthy, died very suddenly at her home in the Ketchum Block Monday night [April 18], it is supposed from heart failure. She was well as usual during the day, and in the evening retired bright and cheerful from a call on Mrs. Ketchum. About midnight she was taken with severe distress and came down to Mrs. Ketchum's room, where she fell upon a lounge, gasped once or twice and was gone. Dr. Bucklyn was called who pronounced life extinct. She was seventy-one years of age, having died on her birthday and on the very hour and minute of her recorded birth.[186]

Another local newspaper noted that Mrs. Langworthy's death "occurred on the eighteenth anniversary of the murder of her son Irvin," which was practically true, the murder having occurred on April 19.[187]

Maria's funeral was held on Thursday, April 21, with the Reverend George H. Miner of the Union Baptist Church again officiating. Professor Bucklyn offered "remarks and read a brief eulogistic poem," and the Reverend Solomon Gale offered a prayer. A quartet made up of Miss Mattie Edgecomb, Miss Sadie Watrous, and Eugene and Frederick Denison "sang appropriate pieces." The *Mystic Press* remarked of Maria: "Mrs. Langworthy was a kind hearted charitable woman, a good neighbor and a devout Christian, with strong convictions she was always ready to maintain." Although the paper reported that the funeral "oc-

---

[186] *Mystic Press,* April 21, 1892. Dr. John Bucklyn Jr. was the son of John K. Bucklyn. He built a house at 58 East Main Street, where he also had his office.

[187] New London *Day*, April 21, 1892.

curred from" Maria's "late residence," it did not specify whether that meant the Ketchum Block or Farmer's Palace.[188]

Because Maria Langworthy did not leave a will, Groton Probate Judge Samuel Clift designated Hamilton as administrator of his mother's estate.[189] At the same time, the judge declared that Courtland, "by reason of weakness of judgment and mental unsoundness, [had] become incapable of managing his affairs" and appointed Frederick Denison conservator for him.[190] The first order of business was to make an inventory to determine the value of Maria's estate, and Hamilton found two trusted local men, John K. Bucklyn of the Mystic Valley Institute and Edward H. Sheffield of Stonington Borough, to act as appraisers. In addition to the properties owned by Maria—the Water Street store, the houses on School Street, and one-third of the Darling Hill farm—the appraisal included stocks, cash, and a major portion of the contents of Farmer's Palace.

The inventory serves as a poignant review of Maria's life as we read down the list. There is the parlor, scene of family funerals, with its chairs, tête à tête sofa, pictures, and Ethelinda's piano. There is Mrs. Langworthy's bedchamber and the adjoining clothes press full of apparel and bedding, where the family claimed they saw Henry's shotgun on Sunday, April 19, 1874. The contents of the kitchen—stove, tables, chairs and curtains—and the items in the kitchen closet are listed with a value of

---

188 *Mystic Press,* April 21, 1892. Gale was the minister of the Third Baptist Church in North Stonington.

189 Town of Groton Probate Records, vol. 10, p. 141.

190 Ibid., p. 148. Frederick Denison was the son of Isaac W. Denison, who lived in Mystic on Broadway at the corner of Washington Street and owned a general store in downtown Mystic. Frederick Denison became proprietor of the store. The Denisons were active in the Union Baptist Church. *Anderson's 1881 Stonington Directory.*

$26.80, insignificant in comparison to the portent assigned to them at William Libby's trial. The sink room where Mary Clarke warned Maria about Libby, the back bedroom where Courtland lay close to death, the woodshed with its saw and hatchet, all bring forth images of the family's tragic past.[191]

One year after Maria Langworthy's death, once her $33.33 share of Courtland's annual support and the appraisers, undertaker, and cemetery had been paid, her estate was settled. In the meantime, Courtland Langworthy had moved to Newport, Rhode Island, to live with his aunt and uncle, Mr. and Mrs. Francis F. Clark. His only possessions, presumably what he had at Mrs. Ketchum's, remained in the custody of Frederick Denison, and those were the meager necessities of one bedroom, including a foot tub, two pitchers, and one glass. In addition to these items, Courtland inherited the two houses on School Street, twelve shares of Washington National Bank (Westerly) stock, five shares of Stonington National Bank stock, cash at Groton Savings Bank in the amount of $960, and deposits at Stonington Savings Bank in the amount of $1,134.

For his part, Hamilton Langworthy claimed the remaining third of the Darling Hill farm, the Water Street store, five shares of Stonington National Bank stock, cash, and the furnishings in his possession at Farmer's Palace. Each son was also willed a sixth of their father's oyster beds in Quiambog Cove, Hamilton already having received two-thirds of the oyster beds when his father died. On paper, each of the brothers' inheritances neatly

---

191 Town of Groton Probate Records, vol. 10, p. 154. The extensive inventory includes a "seal skin sack and muff" appraised at $50 as well as silverware, a gold watch, and three gold rings. The total value of land, stock, cash, and furnishings came to $9,133.90.

added up to the same monetary value.[192]

Once his mother's estate was settled, Hamilton Langworthy apparently set about to realize his dreams. After all, he had been trained as an engineer, and here he was sitting on approximately 140 acres of land along a beautiful hilltop with an expansive view of Fisher's Island Sound and the Atlantic beyond. Several of his neighbors were building large and impressive new houses. In 1891, Maria and Hamilton had sold a thirty-two acre parcel of land along Quiambog Cove to Charles P. Williams Jr., a wealthy resident of New York and Stonington. Williams had built an elegant estate named Stoneridge on the west side of Montauk Avenue with commanding views of the Sound, and he used his new property adjoining the Langworthys' to add more stables, a carriage house, and a half-mile track for trotting races.[193] Hamilton and his mother also sold some of their land east of Farmer's Palace to Aletta P. Horn, who built a summer house named Rocky Ledge.[194] Down the hill on the Stonington side, Gilbert Collins, a New Jersey Supreme Court judge and resident of Jersey City,

---

192 Town of Groton Probate Records, vol. 10, p. 407. Courtland Langworthy seems to have had a boarding arrangement with the Clarks, as an annual accounting by Frederick Denison lists a payment of $72 to Francis Clark for board from January to June, 1893. Town of Groton Probate Records, vol. 10, p. 426.

193 Town of Stonington Land Records, vol. 42, bp. 343. Charles Phelps Williams Jr. owned twenty to thirty horses and a four-in-hand coach. In her *Recollections of Old Stonington*, Anne Atwood Dodge described him as "a large florid, rather imposing looking man, always very well turned out and excessively horsey" p. 15. In 1925 Williams moved to Newport, Rhode Island. He sold Stoneridge, which then became a casino and speakeasy and burned to the ground in 1933.

194 Rocky Ledge is on the north side of Route 1 opposite Lord's Hill Road and is commonly known as "the Daffodil House." Town of Stonington Land Records, vol. 58, p. 120. It is not clear how many acres the Langworthys sold to Mrs. Horn in 1890.

renovated the old Hallam house to reflect the fashionable tastes of the time in a summer estate he called Brookvale.[195] The trend in this part of the town was signaling the disappearance of large family farms and the increase of summer estates and residents. Hamilton's own cousin, Samuel C. Langworthy, decided in March 1892 to stop farming and sell all 140 acres of his land, including Cedar Point, to James Everett Lord, for whom the point was renamed.[196] Lord, who kept sheep grazing on the hillside, later divided the point into building lots for summer cottages. Hamilton, clearly not wanting to be left behind, made plans to leave Farmer's Palace and build his own modern house.

By 1895, Hamilton Langworthy had found a qualified buyer for Farmer's Palace, but the sale did not proceed smoothly. Samuel Doughty, a real estate speculator from Brooklyn, New York, had been looking for a summer home for his family. He was attracted to the old house on Darling Hill and decided to buy it. However, in April 1895 Doughty took legal action against Hamilton "to enforce the performance of a contract." In other words, although a contract to purchase the house had been signed, Hamilton was dragging his heels when it came to the closing. Doughty's legal action described the property in question: "a three story frame house with the plot of ground around it known as the Langworthy place together with all stables, cow barns and all other buildings excepting the corn crib...also part of the orchard... the meadow lot east of the house lot partly occupied now as a

---

195 Wheeler, *Homes of Our Ancestors*, p. 103; Haynes, *Stonington Chronology*, p. 112.

196 Town of Stonington Land Records, vol. 42, p. 419. New London *Day*, April 19, 1892. Samuel C. Langworthy and his wife, Sarah Hancox Langworthy, moved to East Main Street, Mystic, in 1892. Sarah died on April 24, 1893; Samuel lived until he was 83, and died on January 26, 1909. They were survived by two daughters, Prudence L. Danforth (Mrs. J. Romeyn) and Emelise L. Evans (Mrs. Henry W.). *Stonington Mirror*, January 27, 1909.

garden…and the pasture in front of the house to the south of the picket fence."[197]

Perhaps Hamilton was running into construction delays on the new house and could not conveniently move. However, documents in the land records indicate that the problem was of another sort. Apparently, Hamilton had signed over to his brother Courtland one half of Maria Langworthy's third of the farm as security for Courtland's annuity. This arrangement effectively reduced Hamilton's yearly payment to $83.33. Thus, there was a lien on the property, which then had to be released before the sale of the property could be concluded. "To settle all controversy and to secure [his] brother," Hamilton legally changed the security to the Water Street store.[198] This transaction was completed in November, and on December 7, 1895, Hamilton Langworthy sold Farmer's Palace and six-plus acres of land to Samuel Doughty for $6,000. A covenant in this deed specifically prohibited Hamilton from erecting any building within a 350-foot radius of Doughty's house, except in the West Meadow Lot, which was enclosed by stone walls.[199]

Hamilton Langworthy's new house was situated to the west of Farmer's Palace, at the highest point of Darling Hill, commanding "a most extensive view of the surrounding country, eleven lighthouses being plainly seen from the residence, including Montauk Point, Latimer Reef, Race Rock and Ram Island." It had "ten large rooms and an observation tower," and the fifty-

---

197 Town of Stonington Land Records, vol. 44, p. 607.

198 Ibid., vol. 46, pp. 66, 67.

199 Ibid., vol. 46, p. 71. The land conveyed to Doughty was bordered on the east by the Horn land and on the south by the Mystic Road. Hamilton Langworthy's land formed the west boundary as well as the north one, which was only 10 feet north of the horse stable. Town of Stonington Land Records, vol. 44, p. 607.

128 • Peculiar Joys and Peculiar Sorrow

year-old Hamilton certainly did not plan to live in it by himself.²⁰⁰ On May 7, 1896, he married Matilda Clark Stanton. Matilda, or May as she was called, was the daughter of Samuel Morton and Lucretia Palmer Chesebrough Stanton and a direct descendant of at least two of Stonington's founders.²⁰¹ Born September 20, 1877, Matilda was only nineteen when she left the Stanton homestead overlooking Oxecoset Cove in Wequetequock and moved to Darling Hill. Hamilton presented her with a diamond ring, in addition to a large new house with "hot and cold water, plate glass windows, and all modern conveniences."²⁰²

Hamilton was spending a good deal of money, and in the summer of 1896 he took out a mortgage for $2,000 on his new house with the Stonington Savings Bank. The house was furnished with many pieces from Farmer's Palace, but other items, such as an ornate alabaster clock and a marble top table, were newly purchased. The need for more funds resulted in another mortgage in the amount of $1,500, obtained from The Co-operative Building Bank of New York. As collateral, Hamilton put up property on Ash Street in the Borough, which he had purchased ten years earlier, presumably as an investment.²⁰³ In May 1897, Hamilton sold six more acres of land to Samuel Doughty, and in October of the same year, he sold Doughty a small triangular plot

---

200 Grills, *Kith, Kin and Cooks,* p. 424. Form letter signed by John H. Ryan.

201 Ibid., pp. 313, 367. Samuel Morton Stanton (1845-1897) was a descendant of Thomas Stanton (1609-1677); Lucretia Palmer Chesebrough (1843-1895) was a descendant of William Chesebrough (1594-1667).

202 Ibid., pp. 100, 381, 414, 424. In her memories, Matilda refers to the cove as Oxecoset, rather than Wequetequock (p. 100). The Stanton house is on the north side of Stanton Lane at Route 1 and faces the cove.

203 Town of Stonington Land Records, vol. 46, p. 168. The interest on this mortgage was 5 1/5 percent a year. Hamilton Langworthy purchased the easternmost piece of property on Ash Street, with a house and other buildings, in 1886 for $2,000. Town of Stonington Land Records, vol. 41, p. 131.

southwest of the old house.²⁰⁴ Hamilton Langworthy's spending spree happened to coincide with one of the worst depressions this country had ever faced, sparked by a major railroad bankruptcy and the stock market panic of 1893. Nevertheless, the Darling Hill land may have seemed like an unending source of cash. However, despite the mortgages and the two land sales to Doughty, Borough taxes on the Ash Street property as well as the Water Street store went unpaid in 1897.²⁰⁵

Determined to create a handsome country estate, Hamilton Langworthy continued "investing his time and money in improvements, burying boulders, and making solid driveways that [would] defy the ravages of time."²⁰⁶ Besides the house, he had a stable barn constructed and filled it with several cows and heifers, a pure blood Swiss bull, hogs, chickens, four horses, and a number of buggies and carts. Caught up in the racing vogue, Hamilton owned three pedigreed horses: a brown gelding named Skipper, nine years old by Happy Home; a black gelding, Stonington, five years old, by Yulan (this colt promised "great speed"); and a bay mare, Passimette, two years old, by Passion, a descendant on both sides of Hambletonian 10. He also owned a Corning buggy and a Palo Alto buggy, a canopy-top surrey, a sleigh, and a new express wagon.²⁰⁷

Not limiting himself to Darling Hill Farm, Hamilton entered into the life of the community as well. He was an assessor for three years and sat on the Board of Relief for two terms. During the 1890s, when fraternal orders and other organizations became

---

204 Ibid., vol. 45, pp. 304, 412, 478.

205 The Borough put a tax lien of $19.60 on the properties, but it was released in 1898. Town of Stonington Land Records, vol. 46, p. 559.

206 *Biographical Review*, p. 442.

207 Grills, *Kith, Kin and Cooks*, p. 425. Auction flyer, October 30, 1899.

enormously popular, he joined the Knights of Pythias in Mystic and the Stonington Lodge of the Ancient Order of United Workmen (A.O.U.W.), a fraternal insurance society.[208]

HAMILTON AND MATILDA Langworthy's life on Darling Hill seems to have been peaceful and full of promise for the future. On October 9, 1898, Matilda gave birth to a healthy son, Henry Hamilton, and the following spring Matilda found she was pregnant again. However, a sudden accident changed everything. On a Saturday afternoon in October 1899, Hamilton, who had been working in the orchard, fell from a limb of one of the apple trees. The distraught Matilda struggled to drag him all the way into the house. Hamilton proved to be too seriously injured to recover from the fall, and on Wednesday, October 18, shortly after 5 p.m., he died. Those familiar with William Libby's trial might have paused to consider the irony of Hamilton's dying from falling out of an apple tree twenty-six years after Libby had voiced his own concern about precisely the same fate.

Once more, a funeral service was held on Darling Hill, "largely attended," according to the *Stonington Mirror*. The Reverend Henry Clarke officiated, and Hamilton's fellow A.O.U.W members attended as a group. At the interment in Evergreen Cemetery, the A.O.U.W. ritual service was used.[209] J. B. Wilcox, Manuel

---

208 *Biographical Review*, p. 442. A Knights of Pythias Lodge opened in Mystic in 1890 with twenty-one charter members. The A.O.U.W. was founded in 1868 as a fraternal beneficiary society, and in 1897 there were 3,200 lodges. In 1948, its name was changed to Pioneer Mutual Life Insurance.

209 The Langworthy plot at Evergreen (Stonington) Cemetery is distinguished by a very large granite marker with an urn on the top. The family names and dates are listed on it, and around the central marker are small headstones for each member. It is most probable that Hamilton Langworthy was responsible for this elaborate but dignified display. The plot is near the northeast corner of the Coddington Billings Mausoleum.

W. Silva, Frank G. Sylvia, J. B. Coon, William R. Palmer, and Hamilton's neighbor Calvin Wheeler were pallbearers. The *Mirror* gave front page coverage to Hamilton's fall and subsequent death, adding that he was "a popular and esteemed citizen of the town and had many friends."[210]

One can only imagine the shock and grief that overcame Matilda Langworthy. Ten days after Hamilton's funeral and two months prematurely, Matilda gave birth to a baby girl. Although the little Muriel Stanton weighed only two pounds, Matilda managed to keep her alive.[211] Hamilton had not written a will, so the Stonington probate court appointed its own clerk, John H. Ryan, administrator of his estate. By the end of October, Ryan had filed an inventory of all Hamilton's possessions and scheduled an auction of the animals, buggies, farm equipment, and fifty bushels of corn to be held on November 13.[212] According to a newspaper clipping, more than 200 people came to Darling Hill Farm for the auction, and the prices obtained were "good." The horses

---

210 *Stonington Mirror*, October 20, 27, 1899. Calvin Wheeler (1847-1929) bought the Hancox place in the Harbor District from Sarah Hancox Langworthy in 1889. The house is the second house on the left on Wamphassuc Point Road, and the property included most of the hillside on what is now called Rose Lane. This property bordered some of the eastern portion of Hamilton Langworthy's land. Town of Stonington Land Records, vol. 41, p. 537. On October 16, 1899, two days before Hamilton's fall, his uncle Peleg Clarke, age 80, died at his home on Beach Street in Westerly. *Westerly Sun*, October 16, 1899.

211 Muriel Stanton Langworthy was born October 30, 1899 (Town of Stonington Records of Births). According to Muriel's granddaughter Susan Hart, Matilda kept the baby warm in an oven, swaddled inside a wooden shoebox, a nineteenth-century incubator perhaps.

212 Town of Stonington Probate Records, vol. 33, p. 609. Auction flyer, October 30, 1899, in Grills, *Kith, Kin and Cooks*, p. 425. The inventory valued the estate at $17,144. Included in that figure was an old-coin collection, five shares of First National Bank of Stonington stock, and eight shares of stock in the Stonington Building Company, organized in 1891 to construct the velvet mill building on Bayview Avenue.

were sold to Courtland P. Chapman, George Champlin, Herbert W. West, and Theodore D. Palmer, owner of the successful trotter Happy Thought.[213] Montauk Avenue resident Henry M. Palmer and Selectman B. F. Williams also made "extensive purchases."[214] Thus, in a matter of weeks, Matilda Langworthy, unable to remain alone on Darling Hill, found herself back at the Stanton homestead in Wequetequock with her one-year-old son Henry and her tiny baby Muriel.[215]

Gravestone of James Hamilton Langworthy

---

213 Haynes, *Stonington Chronology*, p. 81.
214 Unidentified newspaper clipping, Grills, *Kith, Kin and Cooks*, p. 424.
215 Matilda's mother, Lucretia Chesebrough Stanton, died in 1895, and her father, Samuel Morton Stanton, died in 1897. Her brother, Louis Sayre Stanton (1875-1945), continued to reside at the Stanton homestead.

THE LANGWORTHY FAMILY had been a dominant presence on Darling Hill throughout the nineteenth century, but as the twentieth century dawned, they had all, one by one, disappeared from that extraordinary site. Traces of the family remained in three houses, the barns, stables, and stone walls, but new landowners would claim their own history on these properties. Two forty-acre tracts of Hamilton Langworthy's land were sold to Fanny Noyes Lord in April 1900, adding to the Lords' extensive holdings. One of these pieces was situated between the Stonington road (now Route 1) and the railroad tracks, bordered on the east by Calvin Wheeler's land and on the west by the Lords' land. The other piece was south of the railroad tracks, bordered on the east by Captain Alexander S. Palmer's Wamphassuck Farm, on the west by Lord's Point, and on the south by Fisher's Island Sound.[216]

Hamilton's new house and surrounding land, Darling Hill Farm, was marketed by John Ryan as "the most beautiful spot on the coast between Maine and California." How many prospective buyers looked at the property is unknown, but in 1903, the farm was sold "for the best advantage of all concerned" to Samuel Doughty for $8,000. In addition to the house and its outbuildings on 14 acres, Matilda Langworthy released all interest in Hamilton's oyster beds in Quiambog Cove. The sale also included the 27-acre west mowing lot, where William Libby and the Langworthys had gone so often to collect hay.[217]

---

216 Town of Stonington Land Records, vol. 49, pp. 238, 288. The land north of the railroad tracks sold for $1,200 and the land on the south side for $400, which included seaweed and shore privileges.

217 Ibid., vol. 51, p. 28; vol. 47, p. 475. Hamilton's store at 139 (141) Water Street was sold in 1906 to Jacob Seidner (vol. 51, p. 536). The east lot on Ash Street was sold in 1900 to Mrs. Austin Young. Matilda Langworthy purchased 5 Ash Street from her husband's estate in 1901 (vol. 49, p. 360) and sold it back to Ryan in 1902 (vol. 50, p. 27).

Henry Davis Langworthy's Farmer's Palace was the summer home of the Doughty family for thirty-six years. During that time, the house was renovated and filled with early American antiques. The dining room featured an immense collection of pewter ware. Samuel and Martha Doughty were enthusiastic proponents of the Colonial Revival style, and they dropped the house's old name, Farmer's Palace. Darling Hill Farm seemed more appropriate.

On the afternoon of November 28, 1930, workmen were closing up the old house for the winter and lit a fire in the fireplace "to take the chill off the air." A strong northwest wind was blowing, and "due to a defective flue" a spark ignited the wooden shingles on the roof. Although the Stonington and Hoxie Fire Companies answered the call, the old house burned and collapsed into its foundation in a little over an hour. The firemen even tried to pump water up to the hill from the Lord's Point pond, but to no avail. Volunteer men, women, and children were able to save the pewter pieces and much of the furniture, stowing it all in the barn. The *Stonington Mirror Journal* reported: "More than a thousand people witnessed the fire, despite the bitter cold of the day. Flames could be seen for miles and passengers on board the 'Elizabeth Ann,' inbound from Block Island, could see them soon after leaving, over eighteen miles away."[218]

After this calamity, the Doughtys took over Hamilton Langworthy's new house, which they had previously rented to other summer residents. They remodeled and enlarged Hamilton's original plan to accommodate their children and grandchildren. The Doughtys' daughter, Edna, had married Herbert H. Knox, and their children, John, David, Samuel, and Sylvia, all consid-

---

218 *Stonington Mirror Journal*, December 5, 1930.

ered the farm their home.[219] Fewer and fewer Stonington people would remember the Langworthys on Darling Hill. The murder of Irvin Langworthy, an aberration in Stonington's distinguished past, was an unpleasantness better left forgotten. And by 1948, even local historian Grace Denison Wheeler, referring to Farmer's Palace in her *Memories,* omitted any mention of the Langworthy family.[220]

---

219 Samuel Doughty died in 1931, and Darling Hill Farm was left to his wife, Martha. In 1936, Martha Doughty deeded the farm to her grandchildren, John, David, and Samuel Knox, and their sister, Sylvia Knox Bingham. Town of Stonington Land Records, vol. 71, p. 193; vol. 74, p. 507. For many years, the Doughtys rented Hamilton Langworthy's house to Dr. and Mrs. William H. Robey of Boston.

220 Grace D. Wheeler, *Grace Wheeler's Memories,* p. 121.

EPILOGUE

By 1900, the Langworthys had all departed Darling Hill, but some, of course, were still living. Courtland Langworthy outlived everyone in his immediate family, dying at his home in Avondale, Rhode Island, on January 9, 1906. He was sixty-five years old, and it is unclear how he came to live in Avondale. The *Stonington Mirror* noted that Courtland was the brother of J. Hamilton Langworthy and "for many years was a familiar figure on the Borough streets."[221] He is buried in the family plot at

---

221 *Stonington Mirror*, January 9, 1906.

Stonington (Evergreen) Cemetery. The property that he owned on School Street was left to Hamilton's children, his nieces Maria and Muriel and his nephew, Henry.[222]

The remainder of the Langworthy family story comes directly from a two-volume book put together by Matilda Stanton Langworthy's granddaughter, Phyllis Wheeler Grills. This book, *Kith, Kin and Cooks*, is an eclectic mixture of family histories, genealogies, photographs, and recipes. Picture opening a trunk full of memorabilia in an old Stonington attic! The book has been an invaluable source for this Langworthy history.

Maria Pierce Langworthy, Hamilton's older daughter, seems to have been raised by Briggs or Clarke relatives in Rhode Island, although she certainly may have spent some time with her father on Darling Hill. According to her niece Phyllis Grills, she "attended the Friends Finishing School in Providence and learned the ways of 'The Accomplished Homemaker.'" On May 20, 1903, at the age of seventeen, Maria married Frank A. Sheldon in Stonington. The Sheldons lived in Wequetequock. Marie was only eight and a half years younger than her stepmother, Matilda Stanton Langworthy, and they continued to be lifelong friends.

After Hamilton's death, Matilda Stanton Langworthy brought her two babies back to Wequetequock to live at the Stanton homestead. In 1903, Matilda married James R. Sheldon and she gave birth to another daughter, Ethel May, on June 22, 1904. The Sheldons' marriage did not go well, and the two were divorced. On January 14, 1911, Matilda married again, this time to Charles A. Mell (1877-1965), who had purchased the Isaac Wheeler farm on Taugwonk Road, near Stoney Brook Road. The Mells lived there until 1945, when, after the death of

---

222 Town of Stonington Land Records, vol. 51, p. 578.

Matilda's brother Louis, they moved into the Stanton homestead. Matilda died on January 16, 1959.

Matilda and Hamilton's son, Henry Hamilton Langworthy, went with his sister, Muriel, first to the District 10 schoolhouse in Wequetequock and then the one-room Taugwonk school, walking the two and a half miles each way from the Mell farm. Not thinking that the district school was "sufficient," Matilda arranged for Henry to attend Wheeler School in North Stonington, and he boarded in a dormitory there. Eventually, Henry owned and operated a gasoline station in Old Lyme, Connecticut, for many years before retiring to Florida. He married twice and had one daughter, Ethel May Langworthy. Henry died in 1981 in the Sarasota, Florida, area.

Muriel Stanton Langworthy's memories of growing up in Wequeteqock recall a different time: rowing and crabbing on the cove; the trolley going past their door; the first automobile she saw—Charles P. Williams's open-top car chauffeured by John Shannon, taking the ladies to shop in Westerly on Fridays; walking with her sister Ethel May Sheldon from the Taugwonk farm to North Stonington to take the trolley down to Westerly and then walking to West Broad Street School every day! Muriel, a prize-winning typist, passed the civil service exam and went to Washington, D.C., to work at the War Department in World War I. She returned to Stonington and taught at the Taugwonk School. On September 14, 1918, she married Joseph Alton Wheeler, and they lived in the Paul Wheeler homestead, known as Stoney Brook Farm, on Taugwonk Road. The Wheelers had three children, Henry Langworthy, Phyllis Elaine, and Janice Chesebrough. Muriel Langworthy Wheeler was the first female master of the Stonington Grange, a member of the Stonington Board of Education in the 1930s, and volunteered for the Red Cross and the Defense Council during World War II. Like her mother before her, she was president of the Wequetequock Burying Ground Association for many years. Muriel Langworthy Wheeler, the last Langworthy to be born on Darling Hill, died in 1982.

APPENDIX

Deacon Samuel Langworthy's Will

Town of Stonington Probate Records, Volume 18, page 389
9th day of April 1840

I, Samuel Langworthy of Stonington in the County of New London and State of Connecticut, fully impressed with the uncertainty of life, yet being through divine mercy at the present time in health and of sound disposing mind and memory do make and ordain my last will and testament as follows, viz.

One, I give to my son Samuel Langworthy Junior all the land now occupied by him as a Farm, it being so much of the lands which I bought of Samuel F. Denison as lies North and West of a division line through said lands described as follows commencing on the North where said lands join lands of Robert Denison at a Rock or bottom stone in the wall marked B. and running thence Southerly by the wall of the old Barn lot so called 31 1/4 rods to a jog in the wall near an old Bar way, thence South winding East by a wall 41 rods and 3 links, thence Easterly by a wall 27 rods 5 links, thence South Westerly 26 rods where there is a wall to be made, thence South Easterly by a wall 40 rods thence by a wall that runs through the swamp a little west of South and over a rock in said wall marked B. 71 1/3 rods from thence West by a wall a little over 4 rods and thence South winding West by a crooked wall 42 rods, from thence a little west of South in a direct line about 31 rods to a rock on a little hill marked B. and thence South Easterly 25 rods to the West big Rock on the shore, to him, his Heirs and assigns forever always provided and this devise is on condition that the said Samuel Langworthy Junior shall quit claim to his brother Henry D. Langworthy all the right, title and interest which the said Samuel has in and to the lands which I bought of Lodovic Denison and of Charles P. Williams and afterward deeded to said Samuel and Henry D. excepting the principal Orchard Lot on said lands, and also that the said Samuel shall pay one half of the amount of all debts, annuity and other charges on my Estate herein after ordered to be paid by my Executors.

Second, I give and devise to my son Henry D. Langworthy and to his heirs and assigns forever all the lands now occupied by him as a Farm, it being the residue of the lands which I bought of Samuel F. Denison and lying South and East of the line of division described in the foregoing devise to Samuel Langworthy Junior. Always provided and this devise is on condition that the said Henry D. Langworthy shall quit claim to his brother Samuel Langworthy Jun. all the right, title and interest which he the said Henry D. Langworthy has in or to the principal Orchard Lot, being a part of the land which I bought of Lodovic Denison herein before described, and shall also pay one half of the amount of all debts, annuity and other charges on my Estate herein after ordered to be paid by my Executors.

Third, I give and devise to my son George F. Langworthy and to his heirs and assigns forever my Farm near the Head of Mystic now occupied by said George F. being all the lands not heretofore conveyed by deed, which I bought of George Haley.

Fourth. I give and devise to my sons Samuel Jun. and Henry D. and to their heirs and assigns forever my wood Lot called the

Dean Lot to be equally divided equally between them, share and share alike.

Fifth. I will order and direct that my Executors shall pay all my just debts and funeral expenses and the annuity to my widow according to the terms of the jointure made previous to my Marriage with her.

Sixth. I give, bequeath and devise to my Executors all the residue and remainder of my Estate, real and personal to be equally divided between them share and share alike.

Seventh. I hereby constitute and appoint my sons Samuel Langworthy Junior and Henry D. Langworthy Executors of this my last Will and testament revoking all other wills heretofore made, subscribed or published by me.

In witness whereof I have hereunto set my hand and Seal this 9th day of April 1840.

(signed) Samuel Langworthy

Inventory
Estate of Deacon Samuel Langworthy
Date: September 6, 1853
Inventory, Personal Estate

1 large Bible	1.00
1 Hat	.50
Wearing Apparel	10.00
1 Feather Bed	8.00
4 coverlets	5.00
4 wool blankets	2.00

1 pr Linen Sheets	
1 pr Cotton	1.00
3 large Silver Spoons	5.00
4 Teaspoons	2.00
1 Chest and three Staffs	1.00
3 flag Seat Chairs	1.50
3 wood "	.75
1 Looking Glass	3.00
3 1/2 tons Lackawanna Coal In two bins in the cellar At five 30/100 Dols. per ton (to be weighed)	18.55
	59.30

BIBLIOGRAPHY

Biographical Review, Containing Life Sketches of Leading Citizens of New London County, Conn., vol. 26. Boston: Biographical Review Publishing Co., 1898.

Chesebro, Lydia Fellowes Langworthy. Diary, transcribed by her niece Elizabeth Grant Meacham. Courtesy of Mary Thacher.

Comrie, Marilyn, and Carol Kimball. *The Union Baptist Church of Mystic, Connecticut: Its Story.* 1987. (Copy in Mystic-Noank Library, Mystic Connecticut)

Cooney, Ralph Bolton. *Westerly's Oldest Witness.* Westerly, Rhode Island: The Washington Trust Company, 1950.

Dodge, Anne Atwood. *Recollections of Old Stonington.* Stonington, Connecticut: The Pequot Press, 1966.

Grant, Ellsworth S. *The Miracle of Connecticut.* Hartford: The Connecticut Historical Society, 1992.

Grills, Phyllis Wheeler, ed. *Kith, Kin and Cooks.* Ledyard, Connecticut, 1989.

Halttunen, Karen. *Murder Most Foul, The Killer and the American Gothic Imagination.* Cambridge: Harvard University Press, 1998.

Haynes, Williams. *Stonington Chronology: 1649-1949. Being a Year-by-Year Record of the American Way of Life in a Connecticut Town.* Stonington, Connecticut: The Pequot Press, 1949.

Hurd, D. Hamilton, ed. *History of New London County, Conn., with Biographical Sketches*. 2 vols. Philadelphia: J.W. Lewis & Co., 1882.

Jones, Richard M. "Stonington Borough: A Connecticut Seaport in the Nineteenth Century." Doctoral dissertation, City University of New York, 1976.

Langworthy, William Franklin, *The Langworthy Family: Some Descendants of Andrew and Rachel (Hubbard) Langworthy who were married at Newport, Rhode Island*. Hamilton, New York: William F. & Orthello S. Langworthy, 1941.

Libby, Charles Thornton. *The Libby Family in America 1602-1881*. Portland, Maine: Quintin Publications, 1882.

Little, George Thomas. *Genealogy and Family History of the State of Maine*. New York: Lewis Historical Publishing Company, 1909.

Peterson, William N. *"Mystic Built:" Ships and Shipyards of the Mystic River*. Mystic, Connecticut: Mystic Seaport Museum, 1989.

Roth, David M. *Connecticut: A Bicentennial History*. New York: W.W. Norton & Company, 1979.

Stanton, William A. *A Record Genealogical, Biographical, Statistical, of Thomas Stanton, of Connecticut, and His Descendants. 1635-1891*. Albany, New York: Joel Munsell's Sons Publishers, 1891.

Steenburg, Nancy Hathaway. *Children and the Criminal Law in Connecticut, 1635–1855: Changing Perceptions of Childhood*. New York: Routledge, 2005.

Stone, Gregory N. *The Day Paper: The Story of One of America's Last Independent Newspapers*. New London, Connecticut: The Day Publishing Company, 2000.

Van Dusen, Albert E. *Connecticut*. New York: Random House, 1961.

Wheeler, Grace Denison. *The Homes of Our Ancestors in Stonington, Conn.* Salem, Massachusetts: Newcomb and Gauss, 1903.

Wheeler, Richard Anson. *History of the Town of Stonington, County of New London, Connecticut from Its First Settlement in 1649 to 1900, with a Genealogical Register of Stonington Families.* Mystic: Lawrence Verry, Inc., 1966 (1900).

Articles

Boylan, James. "Stonington's Forgotten Heroes of 1861-65." *Historical Footnotes* (quarterly publication of the Stonington, Connecticut, Historical Society) 37 (May 2000).

Cheseborough, Rev. Amos. "Stonington in the Days of Yore–Part II." *Historical Footnotes* 23 (May 1986).

Kimball, Carol W. "Historic Glimpses: Mystic Valley Institute Emphasized the Classics." *The Day* (New London, Connecticut), July 10, 1986.

Palmer, Henry R., Jr. "The Arsonists." *Historical Footnotes* 14 (November 1977).

———. "The Temperance Crusades." *Historical Footnotes* 40 (May 2003).

Steenburg, Nancy H. "Murder and Minors: Changing Standards in the Criminal Law of Connecticut, 1650–1853." *Connecticut History* 41 (Fall 2002), 125-43.

Public Records and Reference Works

Allyn's New London Directory. 1874-1875.

Anderson's Stonington Directory, 1881.

Atlas of New London County (including Westerly, Rhode Island). New York: F.W. Beers, 1868.

Divorces 1719-1875. Superior Court Records of the County of New London.

Lewiston (Maine). 1880.

Lewiston, Maine, Town Records 1852-63. Vol. 2: Vital Records Prior to 1865.

Lewiston-Auburn (Maine) *Directory*. 1874-75.

Maine Register. 1874.

New London County Superior Court Cases and Files, 1868-1881. Records: Judicial Department, State of Connecticut.

Old Military and Civil Records, Record Group 24, Records of the Bureau of Naval Personnel, National Archives.

Town and City Atlas, State of Connecticut. Boston: D.H. Hurd & Co., 1893.

Town of Groton, Connecticut. Probate Records.

Town of Stonington, Connecticut. Assessor's Records
——. Land Records.
——. Probate Records.
——. Registration of Marriages.
——. Vital Records.

Union Baptist Church. Records, 7 and 8: 1861-1910, Connecticut State Library.

Newspapers

Hartford Times.

Lewiston Evening Journal. Lewiston, Maine.

Mystic Press.

Narragansett Weekly. Westerly, Rhode Island.

New London Evening Telegram.

New York Times.

Stonington Mirror.

The Day. New London, Connecticut.

Westerly Sun.